Biology
The Web of Life

- -

UNIT 4 REVIEW MODULE

Scott Foresman
Addison Wesley

Editorial Offices: Menlo Park, California • Glenview, Illinois
Sales Offices: Reading, Massachusetts • Atlanta, Georgia • Glenview, Illinois •
Carrollton, Texas • Menlo Park, California

http://www.sf.aw.com
http://www.biosurf.com

To the Teacher

Each Unit Review Module contains Section Reviews, Activity Recordsheets, Interpreting Graphics Exercises, Critical Thinking Exercises, Enrichment Topics, Vocabulary Reviews, Tests, and Lab Practical Exams. The components of the Unit Review Module can be photocopied and distributed to students.

- The Section Reviews offer students the opportunity to review the content and concepts in each numbered section of the Student Edition.

- Activity Recordsheets provide students with space to record data and answer questions presented in the *Lab Zone Do It* and *Investigate It* activities in the Student Edition.

- The Interpreting Graphics exercises challenge students to analyze processes, data, or information presented graphically.

- The Critical Thinking Exercises apply one or more critical thinking skills, many of which are described in the Reference Bank of the Student Edition. Students of all levels, backgrounds and abilities can benefit from practicing the thinking skills presented in these worksheets.

- The Enrichment Topics are essays that expand on topics from the Student Edition, by applying underlying concepts to real-world problems. Each topic has an open-ended evaluation section that promotes critical thinking, writing skills, and creative problem solving.

- The Vocabulary Reviews give students the opportunity to review key vocabulary terms while completing a variety of different exercises.

- There are two tests for each chapter. Test A has 25 multiple choice questions that test students' understanding of key terms, content, and concepts. Test B offers questions that challenge students to explain, describe, compare, interpret, and apply higher order thinking skills.

- The Lab Practical Exams enable teachers to assess the laboratory skills of students, to provide an alternative means to assess the progress of students, and to give students the opportunity to demonstrate what they have learned during their laboratory sessions.

Cover Photograph: Tim Davis / Davis-Lynn Images

Printed in the United States of America. Published simultaneously in Canada.

ISBN 0-201-32119-X

1 2 3 4 5 6 7 8 9 10 ML 01 00 99 98 97

Contents

■ ■

Section	Student Activities/Features	Teacher's Resource Package
14.1 Characteristics of Viruses **Objectives** ■ Identify the structural characteristics of viruses ■ Compare forms of viral replication	**Lab Zone Discover It!** *Imitating the Spread of a Virus,* p. 325 **Everyday Biology** *Sick Computers?* p. 329	**Unit 4 Review Module** ■ Section Review 14.1 ■ Interpreting Graphics 14 **Laboratory Manual,** Lab 24: "Tobacco Mosaic Virus"
14.2 Origin and Diversity of Viruses **Objectives** ■ Explain one hypothesis about the origin of viruses ■ Compare and contrast methods for classifying viruses	**Lab Zone Do It!** *Model a Bacteriophage,* p. 332 **Everyday Biology** *The All-Too-Common Cold,* p. 333	**Unit 4 Review Module** ■ Section Review 14.2 ■ Activity Recordsheet 14-1
14.3 Viruses in the Biosphere **Objectives** ■ Describe the role of viruses in the environment ■ Explain viral diseases and uses of viruses	**Lab Zone Think About It!** *Analyzing Disease Occurrence,* p. 334 **STS: Frontiers in Biology** *Human Uses,* p. 335	**Unit 4 Review Module** ■ Section Review 14.3 ■ Critical Thinking Exercise 14 ■ Enrichment Topic 14-1 **Issues and Decision Making** 14-1 **Consumer Applications** 14-1
14.4 Characteristics of Monerans **Objectives** ■ Identify the structural characteristics of monerans ■ Compare how monerans grow, reproduce, and survive	**Lab Zone Investigate It!** *Does Temperature Affect Bacterial Growth?* p. 339	**Unit 4 Review Module** ■ Section Review 14.4 ■ Activity Recordsheet 14-2
14.5 Origin and Diversity of Monerans **Objectives** ■ Analyze the evolution and classification of monerans ■ Compare and contrast methods of classifying monerans	**Lab Zone Do It!** *Identify Shapes of Bacteria,* p. 343	**Unit 4 Review Module** ■ Section Review 14.5 ■ Activity Recordsheet 14-3 **Laboratory Manual,** Lab 25: "Gram Stain: Positive Identification"
14.6 Monerans in the Biosphere **Objectives** ■ Describe the ecological role of bacteria in the environment ■ Explain how monerans affect humans	**Everyday Biology** *In the Bacteria Cafeteria,* p. 344 **In the Community** *Beefing Up Inspections,* p. 345 **STS: Frontiers in Biology** *Employing Bacteria,* p.345	**Unit 4 Review Module** ■ Section Review 14.6 ■ Enrichment Topic 14-2 ■ Vocabulary Review 14 ■ Chapter 14 Tests **Laboratory Manual,** Lab 26: "Familiar Bactericides and Bacteriostatic Agents" **Consumer Applications** 14-2 **Issues and Decision Making** 14-2

Technology Resources

Internet Connections

Within this chapter, you will see the logo. If you and your students have access to the Internet, the following URL address will provide various Internet connections that are related to topics and features presented in this chapter:

http://microorganisms.biosurf.com

You can also find relevant chapter material at **The Biology Place** address:

http://www.biology.com

CD-ROMs

Biología: la teleraña de la vida, (Spanish Student Edition) Chapter 14
Teacher's Resource Planner, Chapter 14 Supplements
TestWorks CD-ROM
■ Chapter 14 Tests

Videodiscs

Animated Biological Concepts Videodiscs
■ Lytic and Lysogenic Cycles

Overhead Transparencies

■ An Influenza Virus, #28
■ Viral Replication, #29 and 30
■ A Typical Moneran, #31

Videotapes

Biology Alive! Video Series
Rewind: The Web of Life Reteach Videos

Planning for Activities

STUDENT EDITION

Lab Zone Do It!
p. 332
- toothpicks
- pipe cleaners
- string
- clear plastic food wrap

Lab Zone Investigate It! p. 339
- three sterile agar plates (per group of 3 students)
- clock
- hand lens
- paper and pencil

Lab Zone Do It!
p. 343
- microscope
- three numbered slides of bacteria (cocci, bacilli, and spirilla)

TEACHER'S EDITION

Teacher Demo, p. 330
Wilting leaves of a plant
- wilting, discolored leaf from a plant

Quick Activity, p. 334
Illness and cause of illness
- overhead transparency
- overhead projector

Quick Activity, p. 336
Identifying moneran cells
- pictures of a plant cell, an animal cell, a fungal cell, a protist cell, and two or three moneran cells

Quick Activity, p. 340
Classifying monerans
- pictures of different kinds of monerans

Teacher Demo, p. 342
Shapes of bacteria
- marble
- piece of rice
- piece of rotini
- overhead projector

Teacher Demo, p. 344
Products made by bacteria
- yogurt container
- can of sauerkraut
- package of Swiss cheese
- jar of vinegar

Characteristics of Viruses
Section Review

14.1

Big Idea!
Viruses are particles that depend on living things to replicate. 14.1–14.3

Ideas
- A virus has a core of nucleic acid—either DNA or RNA (never both)—and a protective capsid.
- A virus can be active and replicate only inside a host cell.
- Viruses can replicate immediately (lytic cycle) or after a period of time (lysogenic cycle).

Words
virus   capsid   envelope   host   lytic cycle   lysogenic cycle   prophage

PART A   *Complete the following for the virus shown in the diagram.*

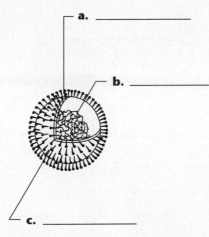

a. _____

b. _____

c. _____

1. Label each of the lettered parts of the virus on the lines provided.

2. What is a capsid?

_____

_____

3. Of what material is a capsid composed?

_____

_____

4. Of what materials is the envelope present in some animal viruses composed?

_____

_____

5. What types of substances are present in the core of a virus?

_____

_____

6. What is the function of spikes on a virus?

_____

_____

_____

PART B   *The steps involved in one method of viral replication are shown in diagrams. Place the steps in the correct order by writing the letters of the diagrams on the lines provided.*

1. _____

2. _____

3. _____

4. _____

5. _____

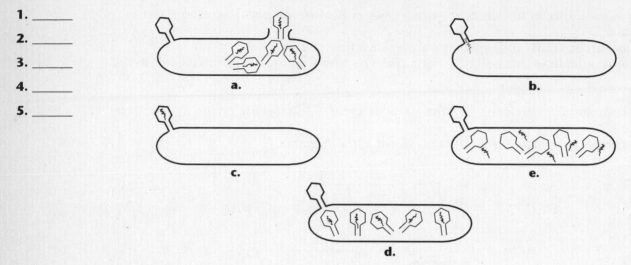

PART C

1. What is a prophage?

_____

_____

_____

2. What happens to a cell when it lyses?

_____

_____

_____

3. How does the lytic cycle differs from the lysogenic cycle?

_____

_____

_____

_____

_____

_____

_____

_____

8   *Unit 4 Review Module*

Interpreting Graphics

Figure 1

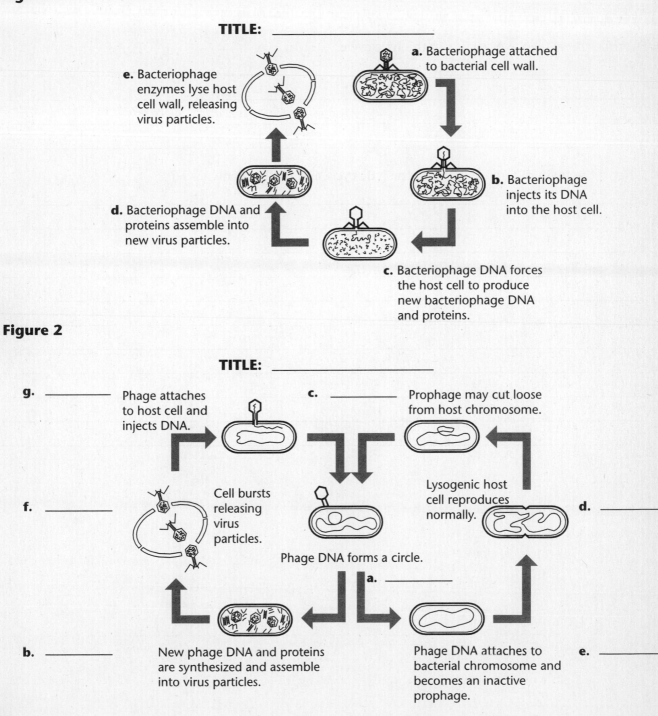

TITLE: _____

a. Bacteriophage attached to bacterial cell wall.

b. Bacteriophage injects its DNA into the host cell.

c. Bacteriophage DNA forces the host cell to produce new bacteriophage DNA and proteins.

d. Bacteriophage DNA and proteins assemble into new virus particles.

e. Bacteriophage enzymes lyse host cell wall, releasing virus particles.

Figure 2

TITLE: _____

g. _____ Phage attaches to host cell and injects DNA.

c. _____ Prophage may cut loose from host chromosome.

Lysogenic host cell reproduces normally.

d. _____

f. _____ Cell bursts releasing virus particles.

Phage DNA forms a circle.

a. _____

b. _____ New phage DNA and proteins are synthesized and assemble into virus particles.

Phage DNA attaches to bacterial chromosome and becomes an inactive prophage.

e. _____

PART A *Complete the following on the diagrams.*

1. Write a title for each diagram that identifies the type of viral replication shown.

2. Write the numbers 1 through 7 on the lines provided to show the sequence of stages in the lysogenic cycle.

3. Circle the stage in the lysogenic cycle in which the bacteriophage is called a prophage.

PART B *Answer the following questions about viral replication.*

1. Describe the sequence of events in the lytic cycle.

_____

_____

_____

_____

2. What is the main difference between the lytic cycle and the lysogenic cycle?

_____

_____

_____

_____

_____

_____

_____

_____

_____

_____

_____

Origin and Diversity of Viruses
Section Review

14.2

. . . .

Big Idea!

Viruses are particles that depend on living things to replicate. 14.1–14.3

Ideas

- Viruses probably appeared after cells evolved.
- Viruses can be divided into groups based on the type of nucleic acid they contain, their shape, and the type of host they infect.
- Retroviruses, unlike any other organisms, make DNA from RNA.

Words

retrovirus   viroid   prion

PART A   *Identify each scientist's contribution to the discovery of viruses on the lines provided.*

1. Martinus Beijerinck

_____

_____

2. Dmitri Ivanovsky

_____

_____

3. Wendell M. Stanley

_____

_____

_____

_____

PART B

1. What was the name of the virus studied by the scientists named in Part A?

_____

_____

2. What invention allowed scientists to see viruses?

_____

3. How does the meaning of the name *virus* relate to the effect most viruses have on living things?

_____

_____

_____

4. What does the current hypothesis about the origin of viruses state?

_____

_____

_____

_____

PART C *Label the parts of the human immunodeficiency virus shown in the diagram.*

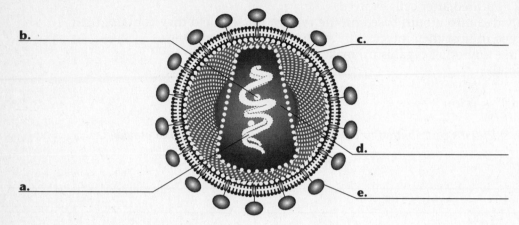

b. _____

c. _____

d. _____

a. _____

e. _____

PART D

1. How do viroids differ from prions?

_____

_____

2. How do viroids and prions differ from viruses?

_____

_____

3. How do retroviruses differ from other viruses?

_____

_____

_____

_____

_____

_____

Do It! Model a Bacteriophage
Activity Recordsheet

14-1

- -

Building a model gives you an idea of structure. You can model a bacteriophage, which is a binal virus, if you. . .

Try This

1. Study the illustration of the binal virus on page 331.

2. Gather any materials that will help you to build your model. These might include toothpicks, pipe cleaners, string, and clear plastic food wrap.

3. Build your model, trying to keep the sizes of the parts in relative proportion.

Analyze Your Data

1. Label the bacteriophage parts on your model.

   _____

   _____

   _____

2. How is your model similar to or different from the models that other students have made? How could you improve yours?

   _____

   _____

   _____

   _____

3. What would you change to make a model of a different virus?

   _____

   _____

   _____

   _____

   _____

   _____

Viruses in the Biosphere

Section Review

14.3

Big Idea!

Viruses are particles that depend on living things to replicate. 14.1–14.3

Ideas

- Viruses can affect plants and animals, including humans.
- Viruses may invade and destroy host cells.
- Viruses are used in making vaccines, in genetic engineering, and in pest control.

Word

vaccination

PART A   *Complete the following.*

1. Name three diseases of humans that are caused by viruses.

_____

_____

_____

2. Name three diseases of animals that are caused by viruses.

_____

_____

_____

3. Explain how vaccination works.

_____

_____

_____

_____

PART B *Explain how viruses and genetic engineering are used to correct genetic defects.*

_____

_____

_____

_____

_____

_____

_____

_____

_____

_____

_____

_____

_____

_____

_____

_____

_____

_____

_____

_____

_____

_____

_____

_____

_____

One Big Bacterium
Critical Thinking 14
■ ■

THE SKILL: Checking Assumptions

An assumption is a conclusion based on past experiences with similar situations. Assumptions are often accepted without direct evidence. Some assumptions are valid and reasonable. Others are false and cause misconceptions.

What image comes to mind when you hear the term *bacterium?* You probably envision a microscopic organism. However, recent findings have disproved the assumption that all bacteria are microscopic. In 1985, a group of scientists studying sturgeon (a family of fishes) discovered a strange single-celled organism living in the fish's digestive tract. The organism was the same size as a hyphen in a newspaper—very large by bacterial standards. Researchers assumed the organism was some type of algae or protozoan because it could be seen with the unaided eye. Classification of the organism, called *Epulopiscium fishelsoni,* proved elusive for many years. Recently, researchers at Indiana University in Bloomington unearthed new data about *E. fishelsoni.* They isolated the organism's genes and compared its genetic material to that of other known prokaryotes and eukaryotes. Data from this study show that *E. fishelsoni* is indeed a true bacterium, similar to the bacterium that causes botulism. Scientists now hope to learn more about the cell physiology of bacteria by studying this giant organism.

APPLICATION *Write a complete answer to each question. Use an additional piece of paper if necessary.*

1. What assumption did the discovery of *E. fishelsoni* disprove?

_____

_____

2. How did the original assumption affect the classification of *E. fishelsoni?*

_____

_____

3. Research has showed that *E. fishelsoni* is a prokaryote lacking sophisticated structures common to eukaryotes. If you were conducting further investigation of this bacterium, what questions would you attempt to answer through your study?

_____

_____

_____

_____

Vaccines Versus Viruses

Enrichment Topic

14-1

The effectiveness of vaccination is based on the way the body reacts in the antigen-antibody process. An antigen is a foreign substance that induces the body to form antibodies. An antibody is a protein that is produced in response to an antigen.

Antibodies combine with the antigens that originally caused them to be produced. The antibodies prevent the antigen from harming the body. Once the body produces a kind of antibody, that antibody can be produced again in quick response to the same antigen. The quick response to an antigen the second time around is known as acquired immunity.

Inoculation, or active immunization, is the process of creating acquired immunity under controlled circumstances. Inoculation introduces an antigen in order to provoke the production of antibodies. Inoculation could also be considered a deliberate infection, with a mild form of a disease, in order to create immunity against a full-blown attack of the disease.

Immunity from inoculation can last for years. A booster injection is an additional inoculation to boost the response of the body's immune system to a particular antigen. The main problem with active immunization is that it can take a long time for immunity to develop after inoculation. Active immunization may therefore not be effective if a person is exposed to the disease soon after inoculation.

There are three kinds of active immunization. An inoculation can contain dead microbes, live microbes, or toxoids. Dead microbes used for inoculation are microbes that have been killed but will still provoke an antigen-antibody response. Live microbes are modified before they are used for inoculations, so they are practically harmless but can still provoke the production of antibodies. Toxoids are toxins that are modified so they are no longer harmful, but they do induce formation of antibodies.

Vaccines are also distinguished from one another according to the medium or substances that contain the antigens. Some vaccines contain the antigen in a fluid. In other vaccines the antigen adheres to an absorbent substance, so the antigen enters the bloodstream very gradually. Production of the antibody increases just as gradually.

Some viruses are better combated with passive immunity. Passive immunity is achieved when the patient is injected with ready-made antibodies, rather than antigens that stimulate production of antibodies. The antibodies come from an animal or another human who has already produced antibodies against the particular disease. Passive immunity acts quickly, but only lasts for a short time. Passive immunity is best used when the process of active immunity is too slow to protect an individual during the time period he or she needs protection.

EVALUATION *Review the information you have been given about vaccines versus viruses. Then make a model of how active immunity works and how passive immunity works.*

Characteristics of Monerans
Section Review
14.4

∎∎∎

Big Idea!

Monerans are microscopic organisms that lack a membrane-bound nucleus and membrane-bound organelles. 14.4–14.6

Ideas

- Monerans are usually unicellular prokaryotes.
- Monerans reproduce by binary fission or conjugation.
- Monerans can survive harsh conditions by forming endospores.

Words

plasmids   endospores   binary fission   conjugation

PART A   *Match each lettered part of the diagram to its cell structure by writing its letter on the line provided.*

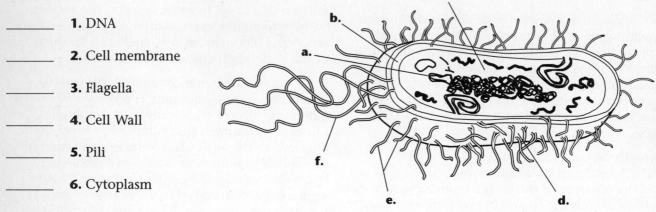

_____ **1.** DNA

_____ **2.** Cell membrane

_____ **3.** Flagella

_____ **4.** Cell Wall

_____ **5.** Pili

_____ **6.** Cytoplasm

PART B   *Match each term in Column B with its description in Column A by writing its letter on the*

COLUMN A

_____ **1.** small pieces of circular DNA

_____ **2.** chromosome replication, followed by cell division

_____ **3.** picking up and incorporating DNA from dead bacterial cells

_____ **4.** special, dehydrated cell formed when conditions are unfavorable

_____ **5.** exchange of genetic material through cell-to-cell contact

_____ **6.** hairlike structures on the surface of bacteria

COLUMN B

a. binary fission

b. conjugation

c. endospore

d. transformation

e. pili

f. plasmid

18   *Unit 4 Review Module*

line provided.

PART C *Describe the process of binary fission shown in the diagram. Then answer the questions.*

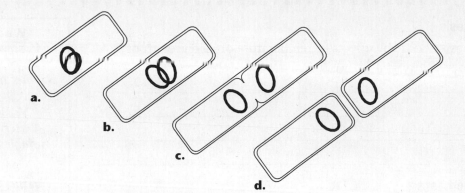

a.

b.

c.

d.

1. a. _____

_____

_____

b. _____

_____

_____

c. _____

_____

_____

d. _____

_____

_____

2. How does binary fission differ from conjugation?

_____

_____

_____

3. What are two ways monerans can share genetic information?

_____

Investigate It! Does Temperature Affect Bacterial Growth?

Activity Recordsheet

14-2

Propose a Hypothesis

Propose a hypothesis about the effects of temperature on the growth of bacteria.

_____

_____

_____

_____

> **What You Will Do**
> *Observe and graph the growth of bacterial colonies at three different temperatures.*
>
> **Skills You Will Use**
> *Observing, controlling variables, collecting and recording data*
>
> **What You Will Need**
> *Three sterile agar plates (per group of three students), a clock, a hand lens*

Conduct Your Experiment

1. Look at the sterile agar plates through the hand lens. They should appear clean with no bacterial growth. Number the plates from 1 to 3.
   CAUTION: Wash your hands with warm water and soap before and after handling the agar plates.

2. Remove the covers from the three plates and expose them all to the air for 20 minutes. Replace the covers.

3. Refrigerate plate 1. Leave plate 2 at room temperature. Incubate plate 3 at 37° C.

4. After 24 hours, examine each plate with a hand lens. In the table below, record the numbers of bacterial colonies at 24 hours for each plate number. Return the plates to the locations described in step 3.

Lab: Does Temperature Affect Bacterial Growth?

I. Objective: To find out if there is a relationship between temperature and bacterial growth.

Number of bacterial colonies

	after 24 hours	after 48 hours
Plate l refrigerated		
Plate 2 room temperature		
Plate 3 37°		

---

5. Repeat step 4.

Analyze Your Data

1. Use the data on your table to create a bar graph of your results. Look at your graph. Which agar plate had the most bacteria after 24 hours?

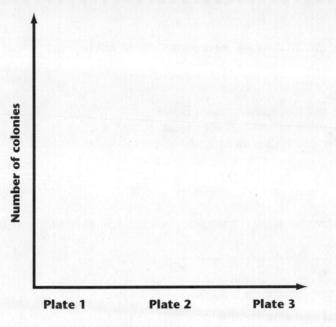

2. Did the same plate have more bacteria after 48 hours?

_____

3. Describe the growth rates on the three plates.

_____

_____

Draw Conclusions

Did your results support your hypothesis? Explain how and why temperature affected the growth of bacteria.

_____

_____

Design a Related Experiment

Think of another single variable, such as exposure to light, that might affect the growth of bacteria. On the lines below, propose a hypothesis about the effects of that variable on the growth of bacteria, and outline an experiment that would test your hypothesis.

_____

_____

_____

_____

_____

Origin and Diversity of Monerans
Section Review

14.5

▪ ▪

Big Idea!

Monerans are microscopic organisms that lack a membrane-bound nucleus and membrane-bound organelles. 14.4–14.6

Ideas

- Monerans probably resemble the first life forms on Earth.
- The kingdom Monera is composed of archaebacteria and eubacteria.
- Monerans can be identified by cell wall structure, shape, metabolism, or respiration.

Words

archaebacteria   eubacteria   aerobes   anaerobes

PART A   *Complete the table by writing the names of the monerans listed in the Data Bank in the appropriate column.*

Data Bank		
cyanobacteria	gram positive	extreme halophiles
chlamydias	proteobacteria	extreme thermophiles
methanogens	spirochetes	

Archaebacteria and Eubacteria Classification

1. Archaebacteria	2. Eubacteria

PART B   *Define each term listed on the lines provided.*

1. archaebacteria

_____

2. eubacteria

_____

3. thermophiles

_____

4. extreme halophiles

_____

5. chemosynthesizers

_____

6. methanogens

_____

_____

PART C

1. How do gram-positive bacteria differ from gram-negative bacteria?

_____

_____

2. How is molecular biology used to classify bacteria according to evolutionary relationships?

_____

_____

_____

PART D   *Complete the following.*

1. List three characteristics used to classify monerans.

_____

_____

2. Explain the importance of the Gram-staining procedure in classifying monerans.

_____

_____

3. How do heterotrophs differ from autotrophs?

_____

_____

4. How do chemoautotrophs differ from photoheterotrophs?

_____

_____

PART E   *In the space below, draw shapes to represent a bacillus, a spirillum, and a coccus. Label each drawing.*

Do It! Identify Shapes of Bacteria
Activity Recordsheet

14-3

....

You will identify the shapes of bacteria when you. . .

Try This

1. Examine under the microscope each of the three numbered slides your teacher has given you.

2. Make a rough sketch of each bacterium, and classify it as either cocci, bacilli, or spirilla.

_____

_____

_____

_____

_____

_____

_____

Analyze Your Data

1. Uncover the slide labels and check to see that you identified the shapes correctly.

2. How did the appearance of the bacteria under the microscope differ? Did they vary much from the photos of cocci, bacilli, and spirilla in Figure 14.17?

_____

_____

_____

_____

_____

_____

_____

_____

_____

24   *Unit 4 Review Module*

Monerans in the Biosphere

Section Review

14.6

Big Idea!

Monerans are microscopic organisms that lack a membrane-bound nucleus and membrane-bound organelles. 14.4–14.6

Ideas

- Monerans are vital as decomposers.
- Many monerans live in symbiotic relationships.
- Some monerans cause disease.
- Humans use bacteria in many ways.

Words

decomposers   symbiosis

PART A   *Define the following terms using your own words.*

1. decomposers

_____

_____

2. symbiosis

_____

_____

_____

3. bioremediation

_____

_____

_____

_____

PART B   *Complete the following.*

1. List four diseases of humans that are caused by bacteria.

_____

_____

_____

_____

2. What bacteria did Robert Koch study?

_____

_____

3. Give an example of a symbiotic relationship between bacteria and animals. Explain the benefits of the relationship to the bacteria and the host.

_____

_____

_____

_____

_____

4. Identify five ways humans use bacteria.

_____

_____

_____

_____

_____

_____

_____

_____

_____

_____

_____

Acid-Fast Bacteria
Enrichment Topic

14-2

Almost all bacteria can be classified as gram-positive or gram-negative by a process called Gram staining. Very few bacteria are gram-positive. Most bacteria, yeasts, and fungi are gram-negative. How bacteria respond to the gram-staining procedure can give clues about the nutritive requirements, cell wall composition, and other traits of the bacteria. When treated with a special dye, gram-positive bacteria retain the dye and appear deep violet in color. The gram-negative bacteria become decolorized and will appear red when subjected to another type of stain. The Gram-staining technique can help doctors identify bacteria and choose the correct antibiotics to treat bacterial infections.

Some kinds of bacteria, however, are resistant to staining and decolorization. These bacteria area known as acid-fast bacteria, and are identified by using the acid-fast stain. Since acid-fast bacteria are a major cause of disease, it is particularly important to be able to identify them. The acid-fast bacteria form a homogeneous group composed of the genera *Mycobacterium* and *Nocardia*. Mycobacterium are usually rod-shaped, and are found in soil, water, and animals. Many species are saprophytic (feed on dead organic matter) others cause diseases such as diphtheria, tuberculosis, and leprosy.

Acid-fast bacteria are characterized by a high lipid content. Lipids make up as much as 40 percent of the dry weight of acid-fast bacteria. The liquid part of the tuberculosis bacteria contains phospholipids and waxes. These waxes are the key to testing for acid-fast bacteria. Some of the waxes contain alcohols, as well as a saturated acid called mycolic acid. Mycolic acid is the substrate that reacts to staining procedure. Acid-fastness is related to the dye's greater solubility in the lipids and waxes of the bacteria than in the decolorizing agent.

One method of staining acid-fast bacteria is to expose them to dye, at room temperature, for 18 hours. Once they are stained, they are very difficult to decolorize.

EVALUATION   *Review the information you have been given about acid-fast bacteria. Then answer the following questions.*

1. How are acid-fast bacteria different from other bacteria?

_____

_____

2. The tubercle bacterium is one bacterium in the genus *Mycobacterium*. Research one other acid-fast bacterium. Write a paragraph about the bacterium. Describe what it looks like and what it does.

_____

_____

_____

_____

_____

_____

_____

_____

Vocabulary Review

▪▪

From each group of terms, choose the term that does not belong and then explain your choice.

1. gram-negative, gram-positive, cyanobacteria, pili

_____

_____

2. binary fission, infection, conjugation, reproduction

_____

_____

3. capsid, envelope, endospore, DNA

_____

_____

4. moneran, bacterium, prokaryote, virus

_____

_____

5. moneran, viroid, prion, virus

_____

_____

6. polyhedral, cocci, filovirus, helical

_____

_____

7. binary fission, lytic cycle, lysogenic cycle, replication

_____

_____

8. methanogen, cyanobacteria, thermophile, halophile

_____

_____

9. chemoautotroph, heterotroph, photoautotroph, aerobe

_____

_____

10. Lyme disease, influenza, chicken pox, sickle-cell disease

_____

_____

Viruses and Monerans

Chapter 14

. . . .

Test A

Choose the best answer for each question or statement and write its letter on the line provided.

_____ **1.** A virus is a particle that consists of a core of nucleic acid and a
      a. protein coat   **b.** bacterium   **c.** poison   **d.** crystal

_____ **2.** Envelopes surround and protect
      a. all viruses   **c.** viruses that infect plant cells
      b. viruses that infect animal cells   **d.** nucleic acids within the capsid

_____ **3.** The spikes covering the envelopes of some viruses allow them to
      a. burst capsids   **c.** filter bacteria
      b. attach to cells they infect   **d.** stop protein streams

_____ **4.** All of the following terms describe viral shapes *except*
      a. binal   **b.** helical   **c.** polyhedral   **d.** prophage

_____ **5.** One hypothesis about the origin of viruses is that they evolved from
      a. fungi   **c.** cells of host organisms
      b. minerals   **d.** parasites

_____ **6.** Viruses that infect and kill bacteria are known as
      a. bacteriophages   **c.** nanometers
      b. chromosomal invaders   **d.** site-specific bacteria

_____ **7.** Which characteristic of living things do viruses lack?
      a. independent growth   **c.** DNA
      b. RNA   **d.** protein

_____ **8.** Two cycles in which a virus can infect a host cell are the lysogenic cycle and the
      a. prophage cycle   **b.** lytic cycle   **c.** bacteriophage cycle **d.** prion cycle

_____ **9.** Retroviruses contain all of the following structures *except*
      a. DNA   **c.** envelope proteins
      b. reverse transcriptase   **d.** RNA

_____ **10.** When a host cell is rapidly killed by a virus, what type of viral replication cycle has occurred?
      a. lytic cycle   **b.** retrocycle   **c.** lysogenic cycle   **d.** nucleic acid cycle

_____ **11.** Tiny particles of pure RNA that cause diseases in plants are known as
      a. viroids   **b.** bacteriophages   **c.** prions   **d.** retroviruses

_____ **12.** Infecting a person with the weakened form of a virus to prevent disease is called what?
      a. transference   **b.** vaccination   **c.** genetic engineering **d.** replication

      Unit 4 Review Module **29**

_____ **13.** Using viruses to transfer genes from one host cell to another is an example of
    a. genetic engineering   **c.** parasitism
    b. vaccination   **d.** retrovision

_____ **14.** Viruses that replicate nucleic acid in the reverse of the standard way are called
    a. prions   **b.** retroviruses   **c.** genetic engineers   **d.** bacteriophages

_____ **15.** One way viroids and prions differ from viruses is that they have no
    a. RNA   **b.** capsids   **c.** chemistry   **d.** power to cause disease

_____ **16.** Prokaryotes do have a cell membrane but do not have a
    a. nucleus   **b.** ribosome   **c.** single cell   **d.** cell wall

_____ **17.** The archaebacteria that produce methane are called
    a. thermoacidophiles   **c.** eubacteria
    b. extreme halophiles   **d.** methanogens

_____ **18.** Archaebacteria that thrive in very salty conditions, such as the Dead Sea, are called
    a. thermophiles   **c.** cyanobacteria
    b. extreme halophiles   **d.** gram-negative bacteria

_____ **19.** Which of the following is an important tool for classifying eubacteria?
    a. gram stain   **c.** methanogen stain
    b. chromatium stain   **d.** chemosynthesis stain

_____ **20.** How do Rhizobacteria help plants?
    a. through parasitism   **c.** by fixing nitrogen
    b. by producing toxin   **d.** by fixing oxygen

_____ **21.** Whiplike structures used by monerans for movement are called
    a. spheres   **b.** flagella   **c.** spirilla   **d.** pili

_____ **22.** Individual cells of monerans can be spheres, spirals, or
    a. cubes   **b.** flagella   **c.** rods   **d.** plasmids

_____ **23.** The process in which the chromosome of a moneran replicates and the cell divides is called
    a. transduction   **b.** decomposition   **c.** symbiosis   **d.** binary fission

_____ **24.** The bacterial process of exchanging genetic material through cell-to-cell contact is
    a. conjugation   **b.** symbiosis   **c.** transformation   **d.** binary fission

_____ **25.** Which of the following is *not* caused by a virus?
    a. AIDS   **b.** malaria   **c.** chicken pox   **d.** influenza

Viruses and Monerans

Chapter 14

• •

Test B

1. Identify each of the following figures as a virus or moneran and label the parts of the virus or moneran. *(15 points)*

a. _____

b. _____

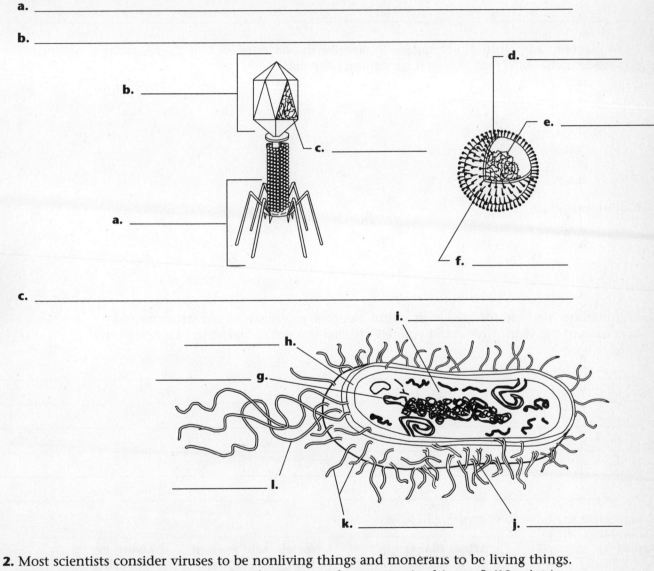

b. _____

c. _____

a. _____

d. _____

e. _____

f. _____

c. _____

i. _____

h. _____

g. _____

l. _____

k. _____

j. _____

2. Most scientists consider viruses to be nonliving things and monerans to be living things. What evidence could you use to classify viruses and monerans in this way? *(10 points)*

_____

_____

_____

_____

_____

_____

3. Describe the process by which a bacteriophage may have evolved from cells of host organisms. What evidence supports this view? *(15 points)*

_____

_____

_____

_____

_____

4. Draw diagrams and write short captions to describe the stages of each of the following processes of viral infection of a host bacterium. *(20 points)*

    a. lytic cycle

    b. lysogenic cycle

5. An organism has been infected with a virus. Suppose you observed the structure and operation of the virus. How could you tell whether it is a standard virus or a retrovirus? *(20 points)*

_____

_____

_____

_____

_____

_____

6. Complete the table to compare. *(20 points)*

Agent	Affect Plants or Animals	Nucleic Acid Present (DNA, RNA, either or neither)	Living or Nonliving
a. virus			
b. viroid			
c. prion			
d. archebacteria			
e. eubacteria			

Section	Student Activities/Features	Teacher's Resource Package
15.1 Characteristics of Protists **Objectives** ■ Compare prokaryotic and eukaryotic cells ■ Explain how protists are classified	**Lab Zone Discover It!** *The Protist Search,* p. 351 **Everyday Biology** *Don't Drink the Water!* p. 353 **Lab Zone Do It**! *Can You Find Protists in Pond Water?* p. 354	**Unit 4 Review Module** ■ Section Review 15.1 ■ Activity Recordsheet 15-1
15.2 Animal-like Protists— Protozoans **Objectives** ■ Describe common characteristics of protozoans ■ Compare diverse protozoans	**Lab Zone Think About It!** *Protozoan Excretion,* p. 356	**Unit 4 Review Module** ■ Section Review 15.2 ■ Interpreting Graphics 15 **Laboratory Manual,** Lab 27: "Protozoans: Animal-like Microbes"
15.3 Plantlike Protists— Algae **Objectives** ■ Describe the characteristics of plantlike protists ■ Compare unicellular and multicellular algae		**Unit 4 Review Module** ■ Section Review 15.3 **Consumer Applications** 15.1
15.4 Funguslike Protists— Molds **Objectives** ■ Describe the structural and functional characteristics of funguslike protists ■ Distinguish between the three groups of funguslike protists	**Lab Zone Investigate It!** *Observing Protist Responses to Light,* p. 364	**Unit 4 Review Module** ■ Section Review 15.4 ■ Activity Recordsheet 15-2 ■ Critical Thinking Exercise 15 **Laboratory Manual,** Lab 28: "Algal Blooms"
15.5 Protists in the Biosphere **Objectives** ■ Describe the ecological roles of protists ■ Explain diseases caused by protists and the importance of protists to humans	**In the Community** *A Protist Investigation,* p. 366 **STS: Frontiers in Biology** *Medicines vs. Malaria,* p. 367 **Everyday Biology** *Is There Algae in Your Sundae?* p. 368	**Unit 4 Review Module** ■ Section Review 15.5 ■ Enrichment Topic 15-1 ■ Vocabulary Review 15 ■ Chapter 15 Tests **Issues and Decision Making** 15-1

Technology Resources

Internet Connections

Within this chapter, you will see the  bioSURF logo. If you and your students have access to the Internet, the following URL address will provide various Internet connections that are related to topics and features presented in this chapter:

http://microorganisms.biosurf.com

You can also find relevant chapter material at **The Biology Place** address:

http://www.biology.com

CD-ROMs

Biología: la teleraña de la vida,
(Spanish Student Edition) Chapter 15
Teacher's Resource Planner, Chapter 15
Supplements
TestWorks CD-ROM
■ Chapter 15 Tests

Overhead Transparencies

Life Cycle of a Plasmodium, #32

Videotapes

Biology Alive! Video Series
■ Signs of Life Video
■ The Domain of Life Video
Rewind: The Web of Life Reteach Videos

Planning for Activities

STUDENT EDITION
Lab Zone
Discover It! p. 351
■ abrasive household cleaning product
■ toothpaste carton
■ empty ice cream container
■ dictionary

Lab Zone Do It!
p. 354
■ small, fresh sample of pond water
■ toothpick
■ methyl cellulose
■ microscope slide
■ medicine dropper
■ microscope

Lab Zone
Investigate It! p. 364
■ microscope
■ microscope slides
■ toothpick
■ methyl cellulose
■ *Paramecium* and *Euglena* cultures
■ forceps
■ metric ruler
■ index card

TEACHER'S EDITION
Quick Activity, p. 352
Prokaryotic and eukaryotic cells
■ overhead projector
■ prepared slides or photomicrographs of protists and eukaryotic cells

Teacher Demo, p. 355
Movement of Paramecia and Ameba
■ methyl cellulose
■ culture of *Paramecia* and ameba
■ microprojector

Teacher Demo, p. 357
Movement of a sporozoan
■ small styrofoam ball

Teacher Demo, p. 358
Uses of diatoms
■ tube of toothpaste
■ car polish
■ diatomaceous earth used in pool filters

Teacher Demo, p. 362
Funguslike protist on a dead fish.
■ dead tropical fish
■ jar
■ water

Class Activity, p. 363
Growing mold
■ starch
■ water
■ fresh garden soil

Quick Activity, p. 365
Simulating a baleen whale and phytoplankton
■ fine-tooth comb (nit comb)
■ infant's hair brush
■ wheat germ

Class Activity, p. 368
Examining diatomaceous earth samples
■ sample of diatomaceous earth
■ water
■ slide and coverslip
■ microscope

Characteristics of Protists
Section Review

15.1

The Big Idea!

Protists are a diverse group of eukaryotes that include unicellular and multicellular organisms.
15.1

Concepts

- Protists have eukaryotic cells.
- Protists are diverse; they differ in size, shape, and manner of movement.

PART A *Use the diagrams of the three protists to answer the following questions.*

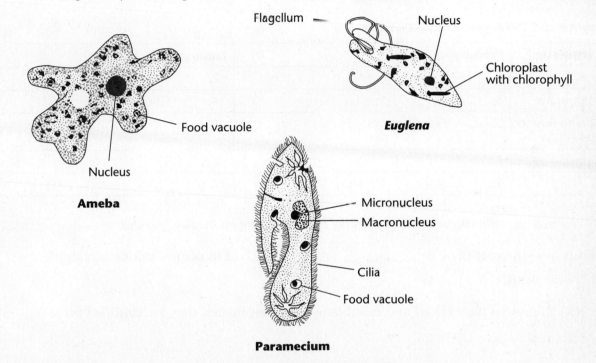

1. What characteristic of each organism indicates that it is not a moneran?

_____

2. Why are the ameba and the paramecium not classified as plants?

_____

_____

3. In what way is the *Euglena* similar to a plant cell? In what ways is it different?

_____

_____

4. How do you know that the *Euglena* is not an animal cell?

_____

5. What characteristics are common to all three organisms?

_____

_____

6. Use your answers to the first five questions to describe protists.

_____

_____

_____

PART B *Compare and contrast prokaryotes and eukaryotes by indicating whether each type of cell has the traits listed in the first column of the table. Write a plus (+) if the cell has the trait or a minus (–) if it does not.*

Prokaryote and Eukaryote Characteristics

Characteristic	Prokaryote	Eukaryote
Nucleus	1.	2.
Cell membrane	3.	4.
Membrane-bound organelles	5.	6.
Ribosomes	7.	8.
DNA	9.	10.

PART C *Complete the following sentences by writing the correct term on the line provided.*

1. Protists live wherever there is _____ , such as in oceans, ponds, and inside other organisms.

2. Because all protists have nuclei and membrane-bound organelles, they are classified as

_____ .

3. A(n) _____ is a group of similar organisms living and growing together.

4. Protists exist in a variety of shapes and sizes. This _____ has made it difficult for scientists to classify them.

5. A popular classification system divides the protists into three groups based on the way they obtain nutrition. The three groups are _____ , _____ , and _____ .

Do It! Can You Find Protists in Pond Water?

Activity Recordsheet

15-1

• •

Observing protists first-hand gives you a better idea of how they move and how plentiful and varied they are. You can do this when you . . .

Try This

1. Bring a small, fresh sample of pond water to class.

2. Use a toothpick to spread a circle of methyl cellulose on a slide, then place a drop of pond water on the slide.

3. Use a microscope to examine the pond water under low power. Sketch the organisms you see, and record how they move.

Analyze Your Data

1. How many different organisms did you observe?

_____

2. Compare the organisms you observed with those in Figure 15.3. Are any of them similar? Are any of them different?

_____

_____

_____

Unit 4 Review Module **37**

Animal-like Protists—Protozoans

Section Review

15.2

∎∎∎

The Big Idea!

Protists can be classified into three groups—protozoans, algae, and molds. 15.2–15.4

Concepts

- Animal-like protists are called protozoans.
- Protozoans are classified by how they move: sarcodinians move by extending lobes of cytoplasm; zooflagellates use flagella to move; ciliophorans live mostly in fresh water and use cilia to move; and sporozoans cannot move themselves.

Words

protozoan   pseudopods   flagella   cilia

PART A   *Match each term in Column B with its description in Column A. Write the letter of the correct term on the line provided.*

COLUMN A   **COLUMN B**

_____ **1.** protists with animal-like characteristics   **a.** cilia

                                                                b. zooflagellates
_____ **2.** protozoans that move by extending lobes of cytoplasm

                                                                c. protozoans
_____ **3.** whiplike structures that aid in the movement of some protozoans   **d.** sarcodinians

                                                                e. sporozoans
_____ **4.** protozoans that use flagella to move

                                                                f. flagella
_____ **5.** short, hairlike projects used for movement by some protozoa

                                                                g. ciliophorans
_____ **6.** protozoans that use cilia to move

_____ **7.** parasitic protozoans characterized by the absence of specialized structures for movement

PART B   *Complete the following definitions by writing the correct term from the Data Bank on the line provided.*

Data Bank		
ameba	paramecium	amebic dysentery
Plasmodium	pseudopods	contractile vacuole
cyst	foraminiferans	

1. Shells of _____ , a type of sarcodinian, form the White Cliffs of Dover.

2. Sarcodinians move by means of "false feet," or _____ .

3. A(n) _____ is a type of sarcodinian with no shell and no distinct shape.

4. An ameba can survive dramatic environmental changes by becoming a

_____ .

5. A(n) _____ enables certain protozoans to expel excess water.

6. The parasitic infection known as _____ is transmitted through water

contaminated by this protozoan.

7. The cilia of a(n) _____ move in unison like the oars of a boat.

8. _____ is a sporozoan that infects blood cells.

PART C   *Complete the following on the lines provided.*

1. On what basis are protozoans classified?

_____

2. Compare and contrast the way sarcodinians, ciliates, and zooflagellates move.

_____

_____

_____

3. Describe the symbiotic relationship between *Trichonympha* and termites.

_____

_____

Interpreting Graphics

. . . .

Protozoans

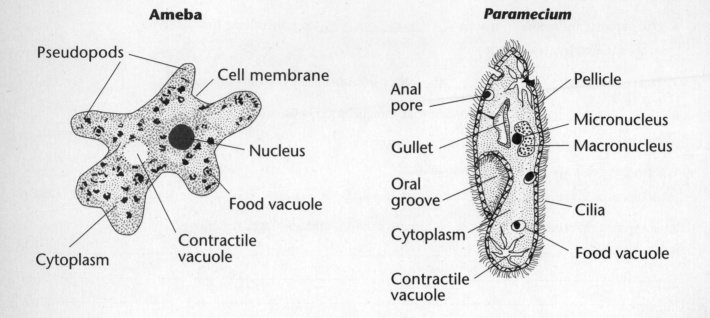

Ameba

Pseudopods

Cell membrane

Nucleus

Food vacuole

Contractile vacuole

Cytoplasm

Paramecium

Anal pore

Pellicle

Micronucleus

Macronucleus

Gullet

Oral groove

Cilia

Cytoplasm

Food vacuole

Contractile vacuole

Euglenoid

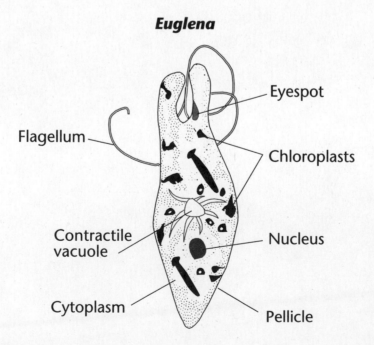

Euglena

Eyespot

Flagellum

Chloroplasts

Contractile vacuole

Nucleus

Cytoplasm

Pellicle

PART A   *What structure(s) are unique to:*

1. the ameba

_____

_____

2. the paramecium

_____

_____

_____

3. the *Euglena*

_____

_____

_____

PART B   *Answer the following questions. Use an additional piece of paper if necessary.*

1. Which two of the organisms are considered to be animal-like? Why?

_____

_____

2. Why is the *Euglena* considered to be both plantlike and animal-like?

_____

_____

_____

3. What characteristics are shared by the *Euglena* and the paramecium?

_____

_____

_____

4. What are the functions of the two nuclei of the paramecium?

_____

_____

_____

Unit 4 Review Module   **41**

Plantlike Protists—Algae
Section Review

15.3

∎ ∎

The Big Idea!
Protists can be classified into three groups—protozoans, algae, and molds. 15.2–15.4

Concepts
- Plantlike protists are called algae.
- Unicellular algae include dinoflagellates, diatoms, and euglenoids.
- Multicellular algae include green algae, red algae, and brown algae.

Words
algae   alternation of generations

PART A

1. Why are some protists considered plantlike?

_____

_____

2. What are the characteristics of algae?

_____

_____

3. How are algae different from plants?

_____

_____

4. What is the basis for the classification of algae into different groups?

_____

_____

5. Into what two major groups are algae divided?

_____

6. Multicellular algae are classified according to what criteria?

_____

NAME _____ CLASS _____ DATE _____

PART B *Complete the following tables.*

Table 1 Unicellular Algae

Algae Type	Characteristic Number 1	Characteristic Number 2	Characteristic Number 3
dinoflagellates	two flagella	1.	2.
3.	glasslike walls that contain silica	contain oil	4
5.	resemble both algae and protozoans	no rigid cell wall	6.

Table 2 Multicellular Algae

Algae Type	Description
7.	This type of algae is usually green and multicellular. Some are colonial.
8.	This type of algae grows mostly in warm salt water. It can be green, red, or black. It can also live where there is little sunlight.
9.	This type of algae grows mostly in cool saltwater habitats and includes giant kelp.

PART C

1. How are red algae adapted for photosynthesis in the light-poor deep ocean?

_____

_____

2. What specialized part do brown algae have? How do the algae benefit from the specialized part?

_____

_____

3. What is meant by the term *alternation of generations?*

_____

_____

_____

Unit 4 Review Module **43**

Funguslike Protists—Molds

Section Review

15.4

・・

The Big Idea!

Protists can be classified into three groups—protozoans, algae, and molds. 15.2–15.4

Concepts

- Funguslike protists are classified as plasmodial slime molds, cellular slime molds, and water molds.
- Plasmodial slime molds have single cells with multiple nuclei that can form spore-producing fruiting bodies.
- Cellular slime molds have single ameboid cells that can come together to form fruiting bodies and produce spores.
- Water molds include different freshwater organisms that act as decomposers and sometimes as parasites.

Words

mold   plasmodium

PART A *Complete the following table.*

Structural and Functional Characteristics of Funguslike Protists

Protist	Structural Characteristics	Functional Characteristics
Plasmodial slime molds	1.	2.
Cellular slime molds	3.	4.
Water molds	5.	6.

PART B

1. How are all funguslike protists alike?

_____

_____

_____

_____

_____

2. Describe the life cycle of a plasmodial slime mold.

_____

_____

_____

_____

_____

3. How is a pseudoplasmodium different from a plasmodium?

_____

_____

_____

_____

_____

4. How are water molds similar to fungi? How are they different?

_____

_____

_____

_____

_____

Investigate It! Observing Protist Responses to Light

Activity Recordsheet   15-2

Propose a Hypothesis

Formulate a hypothesis about what you think will happen when two
different protists—*Paramecium* and *Euglena*—are exposed to light.

_____

_____

_____

_____

What You Will Do

Observe and compare the responses of two different protists to light.

Skills You Will Use

Predicting, observing, collecting and recording data

What You Will Need

Microscope, microscope slides, toothpick, methyl cellulose, Paramecium and Euglena cultures, forceps, metric ruler, index card

Conduct Your Experiment

1. Use a toothpick to spread a small circle of methyl cellulose on the center of a slide. Place a drop of *Paramecium* culture in the ring of methyl cellulose. Using forceps, gently lower a coverslip over the culture.

2. Use the low power lens of a microscope to locate several paramecia. Focus on one *Paramecium* with the high power lens. Examine its characteristics under high power. Record your observations and draw a *Paramecium*.

3. Cut an index card to the same size as a microscope slide. In the center of this strip, cut a slit that is 1.5 centimeters (cm) long and 0.2 cm wide. Slip the strip under the slide on the microscope.

4. After 5 minutes, carefully remove the strip and locate the paramecia. Record your observations in your notebook.

5. Repeat steps 1–4 using the *Euglena*.

Analyze Your Data

1. Describe the characteristics of the two types of protists you observed.

_____

_____

2. Compare the characteristics of both protists.

_____

_____

3. Compare the response of each type of protists to light.

_____

_____

_____

Draw Conclusions

Was your hypothesis correct? If not, why not? If it was incorrect, rephrase it to reflect the results of the experiment.

_____

_____

_____

_____

_____

Design a Related Experiment

On a separate piece of paper, design an experiment to test how paramecia and euglenoids respond to the concentration of salt in a solution. Begin by proposing a hypothesis. Then write out the procedure you would follow to test your hypothesis.

What Are Algae?
Critical Thinking

15

THE SKILL: Organizing and Classifying

Organizing and classifying can help you arrange a large number of facts or items, so that individual items are easier to find, store, or use. In order to organize and classify effectively, you need to identify your reason for organizing. Then you should study the characteristics of your items and organize them into groups and subgroups. When you organize, you will want to review "Observe and Interpret" on page 952 in your textbook.

Algae are difficult to classify. In older classification systems that divided all organisms into plants and animals, algae were usually classified as plants and put in the subkingdom Thallophyta, along with bacteria and fungi. Some algae, however, can move and ingest food. Sometimes these algae are classified in the animal kingdom. In systems that divide organisms into several different kingdoms, algae are sometimes divided among the kingdoms. For example, single-celled algae are placed in the kingdom Protista. Algae with many cells and nuclei have characteristics more like higher plants and are sometimes placed in the kingdom Plantae.

There are many diverse species of algae. Different algae have different cellular structures, pigmentation, nutritional requirements, and numbers and structures of flagella. There are several common types of algae: euglenoids, diatoms, red algae, green algae, dinoflagellates, and brown algae.

APPLICATION *Write a complete answer to each question. Use additional pieces of paper if necessary.*

1. What are some of the criteria used to classify algae?

_____

2. Are algae more like plants or more like animals? Explain your answer.

_____

_____

3. How could you classify and organize a group of algae?

_____

_____

_____

4. Research and describe the types of algae mentioned in the last paragraph.

_____

_____

_____

_____

_____

_____

_____

_____

Protists in the Biosphere
Section Review

15.5

The Big Idea!

Protists have a major ecological impact as food sources, decomposers, and infectious agents. 15.5

Concepts

- Protists in plankton are important in the food chain and in oxygen production.
- Protists cause disease directly and indirectly.
- Protists have many commercial uses including food additives and other household products.

Words

plankton

PART A

1. What are plankton?

_____

_____

2. What are phytoplankton?

_____

_____

3. Why are phytoplankton vital to life on Earth? Give two reasons.

_____

_____

_____

4. How are protists important as a food source for humans?

_____

_____

_____

5. How are protists useful as bioindicators?

_____

_____

_____

PART B   *Identify each part of the life cycle of* Plasmodium *by writing the correct letter next to its term.*

_____ **1.** gametocyte

_____ **2.** zygote

_____ **3.** liver

_____ **4.** merozoite

_____ **5.** gametes

_____ **6.** liver cell

_____ **7.** red blood cells

_____ **8.** sporozoites

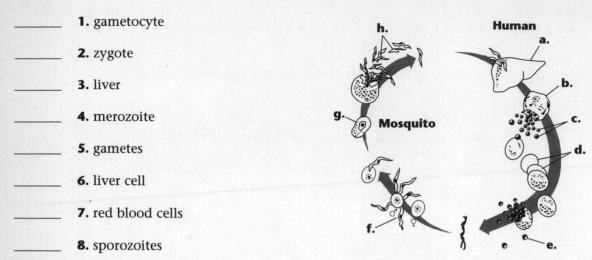

PART C   *Match each protist in Column B to the effect or disease described in Column A.*

COLUMN A

_____ **1.** blight that makes potatoes inedible

_____ **2.** African sleeping sickness

_____ **3.** causes intestinal problems, including diarrhea and nausea

_____ **4.** causes malaria

_____ **5.** producer of paralyzing and sometimes fatal toxin that can be transmitted by contaminated shellfish.

COLUMN B

a. *Plasmodium*

b. *Phytophthora infestans*

c. *Gonyaulax*

d. *Trypanosoma*

e. *Giardia*

Bubonic Plague, A Bacterial Pandemic

Enrichment Topic

15-1

Bacteria have had a great impact on human history. Epidemic disease, in particular, has affected entire populations of people. During Napoleon's withdrawal from Russia in 1812, typhus (caused by typhus bacillus) killed more of his retreating French troops than all the attacks made by the Russian Cossacks.

Many epidemic diseases are spread by insects, rats, or other animals. The spread of disease from animals to humans is called zoonosis. The bubonic plague is a bacterial disease transferred through zoonosis.

Bubonic plague is spread from rats, through rat fleas, to humans. After a flea has fed on blood from an infected rodent, the plague bacillus, *Yersinia pestis*, multiplies in the flea's digestive tract. When the flea bites a human being, the plague bacillus is transferred. The bacteria then travel to the lymph nodes and produce several symptoms, including buboes nodules, the unpleasant affliction for which the disease is named. If the bacteria travel to the lungs, pneumonic plague develops, and the bacilli are coughed up. Coughing can spread pneumonic plague directly from person to person.

Bubonic plague has been the cause of three devastating worldwide epidemics, or pandemics. During the sixth century, an estimated 100 million people in the Middle East, Europe, and Asia died in a pandemic of bubonic plague. During the fourteenth century, an epidemic known as the Black Death killed between one fourth to one half of the population of Europe, about 75 million people. In this period of the Black Death, bubonic plague was transmitted both through zoonosis and through pneumonic plague infections. Throughout the Middle Ages to the seventeenth century, bubonic plague epidemics recurred all across Europe. The plague was carried on ships and in bags of wool that harbored fleas.

Today, bubonic plague can be treated with antibiotics. Small local outbreaks of plague still occur in many regions of the world, even in the United States. The outbreaks have failed to spread into full-blown epidemics, however. This may be because the strains of bacteria alive today are less virulent, and as a result of more modern treatment methods.

EVALUATION   *Review the information you have been given about bubonic plague. Then research one of the topics listed below. Use your research to write a report on a separate piece of paper.*

1. Research the zoonosis stage of bubonic plague. What kind of flea transmitted the disease during the devastating pandemic in Europe? How did the fleas transmit the disease?

   _____

   _____

   _____

2. What kind of animal harbors the plague bacillus today? Research recent outbreaks of the plague and report on potential or known causes.

   _____

   _____

   _____

   _____

   _____

   _____

Vocabulary Review

15

- -

Each clue describes a vocabulary term. Read the clues and write the letters of each term on the lines provided.

1. Clue: diverse group of protists with animal-like characteristics.

— ◯ — — — — — ◯ —

2. Clue: lobes of cytoplasm used by an ameba to move and obtain food.

◯ — — — — — ◯ —

3. Clue: whiplike structures that aid in protozoan movement.

— — — ◯ — — — —

4. Clue: short, hairlike projections that some protozoans use for movement.

— ◯ — ◯ —

5. Clue: photosynthetic protists.

— — ◯ —

6. Clue: life cycle that alternates between the production of spores and the production of gametes. (3 words)

— — ◯ — — — — ◯ — — — —

— — — — — — ◯ — —

7. Clue: microscopic organisms that float near the surface of oceans and lakes.

— — — ◯ ◯ — —

8. Clue: slime mold that is a single cell with many nuclei.

— — ◯ ◯ — — — —

Write the letters found inside the circles on the lines below. Then unscramble them to find the name of the classification for the ameba and slime mold. (The solution is 2 words.)

SCRAMBLED LETTERS:

— — — — — — — — — — — — — — — — — —

SOLUTION:

— — — — — — — — — — — — — —

Protists
Chapter 15

■ ■

Test A

Choose the best answer for each question and write its letter on the line provided.

_____ 1. The only characteristic common to protists is that they are all
   a. eukaryotic organisms   c. algae
   b. monerans   d. unicellular

_____ 2. What protozoan causes malaria?
   a. *Trypanosoma*   b. *Plasmodium*   c. *Paramecium*   d. *Giardia*

_____ 3. Protists are commonly classified as
   a. algae, plankton, and molds
   b. unicellular, multicellular, and noncellular
   c. protozoans, ameba, and paramecia
   d. plantlike, animal-like, and funguslike

_____ 4. What is the term for all protists with animal-like characteristics?
   a. sarcodinians   b. zooflagellates   c. protozoans   d. amebas

_____ 5. Ciliophorans propel themselves through water with their
   a. vacuoles   b. cilia   c. sporozoites   d. flagella

_____ 6. What is the name for protists that perform photosynthesis?
   a. algae   b. sporozoans   c. dinoflagellates   d. ciliates

_____ 7. An ameba can survive harsh conditions by forming a
   a. pseudopod   b. spore   c. diatom   d. cyst

_____ 8. Euglenoids, dinoflagellates, and diatoms are all
   a. multicellular algae   c. green algae
   b. unicellular algae   d. brown algae

_____ 9. A zooflagellate that digests cellulose and lives in termites is
   a. *Entameba histolytica*   c. *Trichonympha*
   b. *Paramecium*   d. *Trypanosoma*

_____ 10. What protozoan causes African sleeping sickness in humans?
   a. *Trypanosoma*   c. *Trichonympha*
   b. *Entameba histolytica*   d. *Plasmodium*

_____ 11. Sarcodinians are protozoans that move by extending lobes of
   a. flagella   b. plasmodium   c. nuclei   d. cytoplasm

_____ 12. The dinoflagellates are a group of algae that
   a. eat small animals   c. make glass cell walls
   b. spin through water   d. have cilia

_____ 13. The extra pigments in red algae allow them to absorb sunlight
   a. from other organisms   c. in deep water
   b. in shady forests   d. at night

_____ **14.** Which organism is a sarcodinian?
    a. *Plasmodium*   **c.** pseudopod
    b. *Trichonympha*   **d.** ameba

_____ **15.** The air bladders of the giant kelp keep the leaflike portion of the kelp near the water's surface to aid in
    a. transportation   **c.** conjugation
    b. photosynthesis   **d.** reproduction

_____ **16.** What protist produces a toxin that concentrates in shellfish, and can paralyze or kill humans?
    a. *Phytophthora infestans*   **c.** *Gonyaulax*
    b. *Trypanosoma*   **d.** *Giardia*

_____ **17.** Two kinds of sarcodinians that have hard shells are radiolarians and
    a. foraminiferans   **c.** ciliates
    b. amebas   **d.** euglenoids

_____ **18.** Algae that lack both cilia and flagella but have cell walls containing silica are called
    a. brown algae   **c.** diatoms
    b. euglenoids   **d.** green algae

_____ **19.** What funguslike protist acts as a decomposer?
    a. autotroph   **c.** spore
    b. mold   **d.** protozoan

_____ **20.** Alternation of generations implies a diploid, spore-producing phase alternating with a(n)
    a. monoploid, bud-producing phase   **c.** asexual phase
    b. sperm-producing phase   **d.** haploid, gamete-producing phase

_____ **21.** Protozoans are classified into four groups according to their
    a. method of movement   **c.** size
    b. method of reproduction   **d.** nutritional requirements

_____ **22.** Organisms that feed on dead organisms or their remains are called
    a. phytoplankton   **c.** euglenoids
    b. sporozoans   **d.** decomposers

_____ **23.** Protozoans that use whiplike structures for movement are called
    a. ciliophorans   **c.** zooflagellates
    b. amebas   **d.** sporozoans

_____ **24.** Which protozoans have no means of movement and live as parasites in animals?
    a. sporozoans   **c.** sarcodinians
    b. dinoflagellates   **d.** *Paramecium*

_____ **25.** What is the feeding stage in the life cycle of a plasmodial slime mold?
    a. zygote   **c.** sporozoite
    b. fungi   **d.** plasmodium

Protists
Chapter 15

● ●

Test B

Read each question or statement and respond on the lines provided.

1. a. What characteristic do all protists have in common? *(5 points)*

_____

_____

b. What classification problem do protists present? *(5 points)*

_____

_____

2. The following table provides information on the three groups into which protists are generally divided. Complete the table. *(18 points)*

Group	Resemble Fungi, Animals, or Plants	Autotrophic, Heterotrophic, or Decomposers
a. protozoans		
b. algae		
c. slime molds		

3. Into what four groups are protozoans divided? How do the organisms in these groups differ from each other in terms of the way they move? Give an example of an organism in each group. *(24 points)*

_____

_____

_____

_____

4. Suppose you are on a scientific expedition to classify algae. Read the following descriptions of algal specimens and state in which group you would classify each. Choose from the following: dinoflagellates, diatoms, euglenoids, green algae, red algae, and brown algae. *(24 points)*

_____ **a.** unicellular, has a flagellum, no cell wall, resembles both algae and protozoa

_____ **b.** multicellular, collected in deep ocean water in the tropics

_____ **c.** unicellular, found floating on the ocean surface, has no cilia or flagella, has a glasslike cell wall

_____ **d.** 50 m long, found in cool ocean water, has air bladders

_____ **e.** unicellular, has two flagella and a cell wall, found in salt water

_____ **f.** found in a pond, is multicellular and green, has flagella

5. a. What are the three groups of funguslike protists? *(6 points)*

_____

b. State one characteristic of each of these groups. *(6 points)*

_____

_____

_____

_____

6. a. Some protists cause disease and illness in humans. State what condition is caused by each of the following: *Plasmodium*, *Giardia*, and *Trypanosoma*. *(6 points)*

_____

_____

_____

b. Describe two important ecological roles played by the protists in plankton. *(6 points)*

_____

_____

_____

_____

Section	Student Activities/Features	Teacher's Resource Package
16.1 Characteristics of Fungi **Objectives** ■ Identify the common characteristics of fungi ■ Describe the structure, nutrition, and growth of typical fungi	**Lab Zone Discover It!** *Grouping Mushrooms,* p. 373 **Lab Zone Think About It!** *Modeling Fungi Growth,* p. 376	**Unit 4 Review Module** ■ Section Review 16.1 **Laboratory Manual,** Lab 29: "Fungi Have Needs, Too"
16.2 Origin and Diversity of Fungi **Objectives** ■ Compare and contrast the group of fungi ■ Describe the reproduction of fungi	**Everyday Biology** *A Shower Smorgasbord,* p. 379 **In the Community** *Pharmacies and Fungi,* p. 383	**Unit 4 Review Module** ■ Section Review 16.2 ■ Interpreting Graphics 16 ■ Critical Thinking Exercise 16 ■ Enrichment Topic 16-1
16.3 Fungi in the Biosphere **Objectives** ■ Describe the role of fungi in the environment and their relationships with other organisms ■ Compare and contrast fungal diseases and appraise the importance of fungi to humans	**Lab Zone Do It!** *Does Moisture Affect Bread Mold Growth?* p. 386 **STS: Frontiers in Biology** *Fungi in Medicine,* p. 387 **Everyday Biology** *A Fungus for a Headache?* p. 387 **Lab Zone Investigate It!** *Comparing Spores of Fungi and Green Plants* p. 388	**Unit 4 Review Module** ■ Section Review 16.3 ■ Activity Recordsheets 16-1 and 16-2 ■ Enrichment Topic 16-2 ■ Vocabulary Review 16 ■ Chapter 16 Tests **Issues and Decision Making** 16-1 **Consumer Applications** 16-1 and 16-2

Technology Resources

Internet Connections

Within this chapter, you will see the bioSURF logo. If you and your students have access to the Internet, the following URL address will provide various Internet connections that are related to topics and features presented in this chapter:

http://microorganisms.biosurf.com

You can also find relevant chapter material at **The Biology Place** address:

http://www.biology.com

CD-ROMs

Biología: la teleraña de la vida, (Spanish Student Edition) Chapter 16
Teacher's Resource Planner, Chapter 16 Supplements
TestWorks CD-ROM
- Chapter 16 Tests

Overhead Transparencies

- Life Cycle of a Common Mold, #33
- Life Cycle of a Club Fungi, #34

Videotapes

Biology Alive! Video Series
Rewind: The Web of Life Reteach Videos

Planning for Activities

STUDENT EDITION
Lab Zone
Discover It! p. 373
- several different varieties of fresh mushrooms

Lab Zone Do It!
  p. 386
- sliced bread
- water
- plastic bags
- plain, rounded toothpicks

Lab Zone
Investigate It! p. 388
- mushroom
- fern frond with spore cases
- single-edged razor blade
- 2 pairs of forceps
- microscope
- microscope slides

TEACHER'S EDITION
Teacher Demo, p. 374
Fungi cells
- microprojector or photographs of yeast cells and fungi cells

Class Activity, p. 376
Modeling absorption of digested food molecules
- thin strips of paper towels
- Petri dishes
- colored water

Teacher Demo, p. 378
Identifying the four fungal divisions
- molded bread
- mushroom
- package of Brewer's yeast
- empty prescription bottle labeled *Penicillin*

Teacher Demo, p. 382
Dissecting a mushroom
- large mushroom
- knife
- hand lens

Class Activity, p. 380
Mushroom spore prints
- mushrooms
- scissors
- small jar
- paper
- jar
- microscope

Teacher Demo, p. 384
Molds in cheese
- Brie cheese

Class Activity, p. 386
Preservatives in food preparation
- water
- commerically pre-pared bread
- fresh baked bread
- plastic bags
- plain, rounded toothpicks

Characteristics of Fungi
Section Review

16.1

▪▪

The Big Idea!
Fungi are stationary organisms that live as heterotrophs 16.2–16.2

Concepts
- Most fungi are multicellular organisms composed of individual filaments called hyphae.
- The bodies of most fungi are composed of interwoven hyphae called mycelia.
- Most fungi absorb the nutrients they need from dead organisms.
- Growth in fungi is usually very rapid because absorbed nutrients are transported to growing areas of hyphae; the hyphae of the mycelium share the same cytoplasm.

Words
hyphae   septa   mycelium

PART A   *Match each term in Column B with its description in Column A. Write the letter of the correct term on the line provided.*

COLUMN A

_____ **1.** walls that divide fungal hyphae into segments

_____ **2.** organism that absorbs nutrients from living hosts, harming the host organism

_____ **3.** organism that digests and absorbs nutrients from dead organisms

_____ **4.** individual filaments containing cytoplasm and nuclei that make up fungi

_____ **5.** mass of interwoven hyphae that make up the body of a fungus

_____ **6.** type of relationship in which an organism absorbs nutrients from living hosts while providing the host with needed materials

COLUMN B

a. hyphae

b. septa

c. mycelium

d. saprophyte

e. parasite

f. mutualistic

PART B   *In the space provided, draw sketches showing the two types of hyphae. Identify the parts of each sketch.*

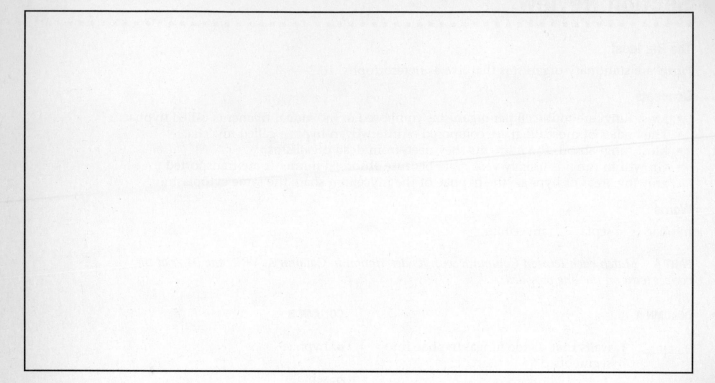

PART C

1. Based on your drawings from Part B, explain how the two types of hyphae differ.

_____

_____

2. Why are fungal mycelia able to grow very quickly?

_____

_____

3. What are the three main parts that make up the body of a mushroom?

_____

_____

4. How do fungi use enzymes to obtain nutrients?

_____

_____

_____

5. How can a cluster of mushrooms actually be a single organism?

_____

_____

Origin and Diversity of Fungi
Section Review

16.2

The Big Idea
Fungi are stationary organisms that live as heterotrophs. 16.1–16.2

Concepts
- Mycologists hypothesize that fungi evolved at least 400 million years ago from an ancestral protist.
- The four divisions of fungi are Zygomycota (common molds); Ascomycota (sac fungi); Basidiomycota (club fungi); Deuteromycota (imperfect fungi).
- Some fungi are classified on the basis of structures used in reproduction: zygospore, ascus, and basidium.

Words
spores   rhizoids   stolons   zygospore   asci   basidia

PART A

1. When did fungi evolve?

_____

2. Why are fungi grouped into a separate kingdom from plants and animals?

_____

_____

_____

3. What is the basis for the classification of fungi into four divisions?

_____

_____

4. How are imperfect fungi different from other types of fungi?

_____

_____

5. What are the four methods of asexual reproduction in fungi?

_____

_____

_____

PART B   *Match each fungal structure in Column B with its description in Column A. Write the letter of the correct structure on the line provided.*

COLUMN A

_____ **1.** haploid reproductive cells that can develop into a new fungus

_____ **2.** specialized hyphae, found in most fungi, that release reproductive cells

_____ **3.** type of spore that can survive for many years in harsh conditions

_____ **4.** saclike structure containing nuclei produced during reproduction of some fungi

_____ **5.** specialized hyphae that transport nutrients throughout the fungus

_____ **6.** spore-producing structure found in club fungi

_____ **7.** rootlike hyphae that absorb nutrients and anchor a fungus to its food source

COLUMN B

a. rhizoids

b. stolons

c. zygospore

d. basidium

e. ascus

f. sporangia

g. spores

PART C   *Complete the table.*

Fungal Divisions

Division	Common Name	Type of Reproduction	Defining Sexual Structure	Example
Ascomycota	sac fungi	1.	2.	3.
Basidiomycota	4.	sexual; rarely asexual	5.	6.
Zygomycota	7.	8.	zygospore	9.
Deuteromycota	10.	11.	12.	*Penicillium*

Interpreting Graphics   16

∙∙

Reproductive Structures of Fungi

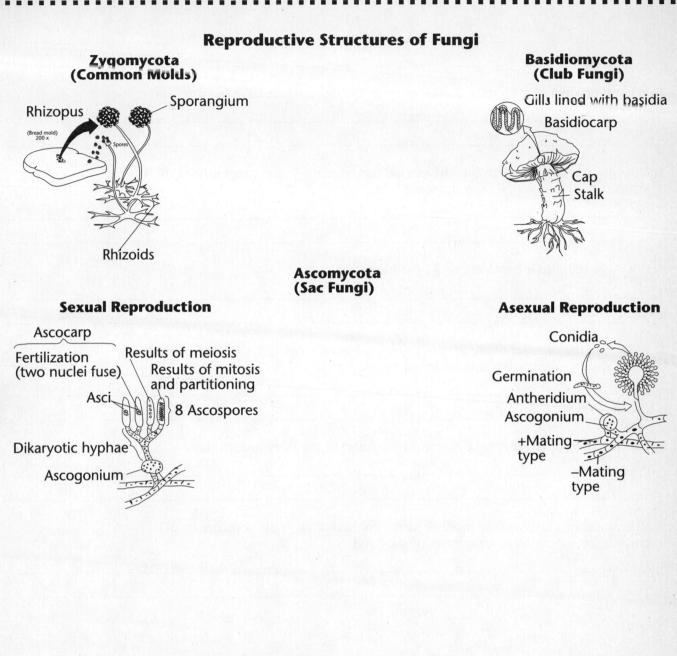

Zygomycota (Common Molds)

Rhizopus
(Bread mold)
200 x

Sporangium

Spores

Rhizoids

Basidiomycota (Club Fungi)

Gills lined with basidia

Basidiocarp

Cap
Stalk

Ascomycota (Sac Fungi)

Sexual Reproduction

Ascocarp

Fertilization (two nuclei fuse)

Results of meiosis

Results of mitosis and partitioning

Asci

8 Ascospores

Dikaryotic hyphae

Ascogonium

Asexual Reproduction

Conidia

Germination

Antheridium

Ascogonium

+Mating type

−Mating type

Answer the following questions on the lines provided.

1. How do the names of the reproductive structures of fungi relate to the names of the classes of fungi?

_____

_____

2. What reproductive structures do the fungi in the illustrations have in common?

_____

_____

3. How do the structures involved in asexual reproduction in sac fungi differ from the structures used in sexual reproduction?

_____

_____

4. What are the plus (+) and minus (–) mating types?

_____

_____

5. How does the number of ascospores resulting from meiosis differ from the number of ascospores resulting from mitosis in sac fungi?

_____

_____

6. How do the imperfect fungi differ from the fungi in the three groups shown?

_____

_____

7. How does the chromosome number in the conidia of sac fungi compare to the chromosome number of ascospores of sac fungi?

_____

_____

Spore Structure
Critical Thinking

THE SKILL: Asking Questions

All scientific investigations seek to answer questions. A good question is one that clearly identifies the type of information being sought. It targets a particular type of response. A good science question also seeks a response that can be clearly observed or measured.

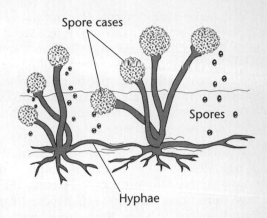

Spore cases

Spores

Hyphae

Many fungi can reproduce both sexually and asexually. Threadlike fungi, such as bread mold, reproduce asexually by spores. Specialized hyphae that grow upward make spores in round black spore cases. When the spore cases break open, millions of spores are released into the surrounding environment. The drawing shows the structure of bread mold. Use the drawing to answer the questions that follow.

APPLICATION *Write a complete answer to each question. Use additional pieces of paper if necessary.*

1. Spore cases can be broken open by wind, animals, insects, or water. List three questions you could ask regarding the structure and characteristics of a spore case.

_____
_____
_____
_____
_____
_____

2. Describe an experiment you could conduct to answer one of the questions you listed in question 1.

_____
_____
_____

3. Once a spore case breaks open, the released spores must land in an environment with suitable moisture, warmth, and food in order for a new fungus to develop. List three questions you could ask to identify which conditions are best for fungal growth.

_____
_____

4. Describe an experiment you could conduct to answer one of the questions you listed in question 3.

_____
_____
_____
_____

Basidiomycota on Your Pizza?

Enrichment Topic

16-1

Do you like Basidiomycota on your pizza? Basidiomycota is a division of fungi, some types of which are edible. *Basidion* is Greek for "small base" and *mykes* means fungus. The basidiomycetes include smuts, rusts, jelly fungi, puffballs, stinkhorns—and mushrooms. There are approximately 25,000 different species of basidiomycetes, some of which are the mushrooms you put on your pizza.

The Basidiomycota are different from all other fungi because they have microscopic, clublike reproductive structures called basidia. Each basidium bears haploid sexual spores, called basidiospores. All basidiomycetes produce a primary and secondary mycelium. The primary (haploid) mycelium is called the monokaryon. The secondary mycelium, the dikaryon, contains pairs of parental nuclei. The parental nuclei replicate by conjugate division.

There are two classes of basidiomycetes. One class, the Homobasidiomycetae, includes two sub-classes. The sub-class Hymenomycetes includes common mushrooms, shelf and coral fungi. The other sub-class, Gasteromycetes, includes the puffballs, earthstars, stinkhorns, and bird's nest fungi. The other class of basidiomycetes is the Heterbasidiomycetae, which includes the jelly fungi, rusts, and smuts.

The spores of many basidiomycetes mature inside a structure called a basidiocarp. The spores are released when the basidiocarp is ruptured or decays. Rusts and smuts produce a spore on the secondary mycelium. This spore produces the basidium. Rusts, smuts, and jelly fungi are parasites. They do not produce fruiting bodies but develop teliospores in the tissues of higher plants. Some rusts cause diseases of cereal crops.

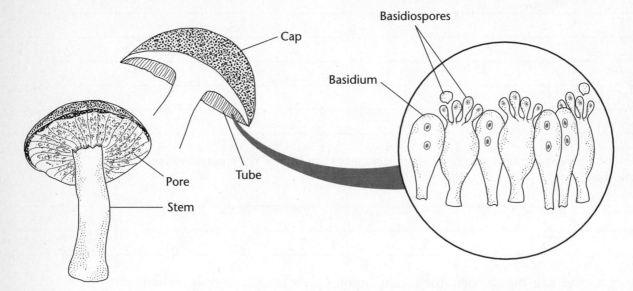

EVALUATION   *Review the information you have been given about the Basidiomycota. Then answer the following questions on a separate piece of paper.*

1. Look at the two illustrations above. They show reproduction of the mushroom *Boletus chrysenteron*. Research the stages of reproduction in basidiomycetes. Write a brief paragraph explaining your findings.

2. How do most basidiomycetes reproduce?

Fungi in the Biosphere
Section Review

16.3

• •

The Big Idea!

Fungi act as decomposers and symbiotic partners of humans and many other organisms. 16.3

Concepts

• Many fungi are decomposers.
• Symbiotic relationships between certain fungi and algae result in lichens.
• Symbiotic relationships between fungi and plants can result in mycorrhizae.
• Fungal disease in plants include smuts, rusts, and Dutch elm disease; fungal diseases in humans include athlete's foot, ringworm, yeast infections, and lung infections.
• Some fungi are important to humans as a source of food, medicines, and eukaryotic cells for genetic engineering applications.

Words

lichen   mycorrhizae

PART A   *Complete the following definitions by writing the correct term on the line provided.*

1. Fungi are important in maintaining a stable ecosystem because they

_____ nutrients and form _____ relationships with other

organisms.

2. A(n) _____ is a relationship between organisms of different species that

live in close contact.

3. Mycorrhizae are a(n) _____ relationship between fungi and plant roots. In

other words, _____ benefit from the relationship.

4. A lichen is the result of a symbiotic relationship between fungi and

_____ . The _____ benefits from the relationship, while

the _____ is unaffected.

PART B   *Complete the following on the lines provided.*

1. Describe how fungi benefit from a mycorrhizal association with plants.

_____

_____

_____

2. Describe how plants benefit from a mycorrhizal relationship with fungi.

_____

_____

_____

3. Explain why lichens are able to grow in harsh environments.

_____

_____

_____

4. Describe how lichens contribute to soil formation.

_____

_____

5. List three types of fungi that affect plants.

_____

_____

6. Explain how Dutch elm disease affects the elm tree.

_____

_____

_____

PART C *List a way in which the following fungi benefit humans.*

1. *Aspergillus*

_____

2. yeast

_____

3. *Penicillium*

_____

Do It! Does Moisture Affect Bread-Mold Growth?
Activity Recordsheet

16-1

You can compare conditions for growing bread mold when you . . .

Try This

1. You need two slices of bread. Moisten the surface of one slice with water, and leave both slices exposed to the classroom air for a few hours.

2. Put a little more water on the moistened slice and place the slices of bread in separate plastic bags. To keep the bags from touching the bread, insert plain, rounded toothpicks in the bread as needed. Seal the bags.

3. After 4 or 5 days, look for mold growing on the bread.

Analyze Your Data

1. Do you see mold? Is there more mold on one slice than on the other?

_____

2. What conclusions can you draw about the effect of moisture on bread-mold growth?

_____

_____

_____

Investigate It! Comparing Spores of Fungi and Green Plants

Activity Recordsheet   16-2

- -

Propose a Hypothesis

How do you think spores from plants compare with spores from fungi?
Propose a hypothesis.

_____

_____

_____

_____

Conduct Your Experiment

1. Use a razor blade and forceps to cut a paper-thin section of a gill from the underside of a mushroom cap, as shown in the photograph. **CAUTION:** Handle the razor blade with care.

2. Prepare a wet mount of the gill section. Examine the slide under a microscope set at low power.

3. Take notes on your observations of the mushroom gill and diagram what you see.

4. Remove a spore case from the fern frond and transfer it to a microscope slide. Examine it at low power.

5. Take notes on your observations of the fern spore case and record what you see.

6. Remove the slide. Using the other pair of forceps, gently pull open the fern spore case.

7. Examine the slide again, and record your observations of the inside of the fern spore case.

Analyze Your Data

1. Describe any similarities you observed in the mushroom and fern spores.

_____

_____

2. Describe any differences you observed in the mushroom and fern spores.

_____

_____

_____

> **What You Will Do**
> *Examine and compare the external reproductive structures and spores of the mushroom and fern and design a related experiment.*
>
> **Skills You Will Use**
> *Observing, collecting and recording data, predicting, experimenting*
>
> **What You Will Need**
> *A mushroom, a fern frond with spore cases, a single-edged razor blade, 2 pairs of forceps, a microscope, 2 microscope slides*

Draw Conclusions

What characteristics were you able to compare in this experiment? From this experiment, what conclusions can you draw about the similarities and differences between the reproductive structures of fungi and ferns?

_____

_____

_____

_____

_____

Design a Related Experiment

Suppose your teacher gives you another spore case and asks you to identify its source as either a mushroom or a fern. On the lines provided, propose a hypothesis, then design an experiment that will test your hypothesis.

_____

_____

_____

_____

_____

_____

_____

_____

_____

_____

_____

_____

_____

_____

_____

_____

_____

_____

_____

_____

_____

_____

Chain and Florey's Penicillin Contribution

Enrichment Topic   16-2

Penicillin was the first modern antibiotic and is still one of the most effective treatments for diseases caused by bacteria. Penicillin is a natural compound produced by the mold *Penicillium notatum*. Penicillin interferes with the growth of the bacterial cell walls, causing them to burst.

Three people were awarded a joint Nobel Prize for their work on the discovery and development of penicillin: Alexander Fleming, Howard W. Florey, and Ernst B. Chain. Alexander Fleming is often credited with the discovery of penicillin, but the importance of his role has been disputed.

Alexander Fleming was a Scottish bacteriologist. During World War I, he performed important research on soldiers and their natural resistance to infection. In 1928, Fleming discovered a penicillin colony growing in a Petri dish in his laboratory. The mold seemed to have inhibited the growth of *Staphylococcus* bacteria. Fleming wrote a paper identifying the mold and its interaction with *Staphylococcus*.

In his paper, Fleming pointed out the effect penicillin has on different gram-positive bacteria, such as *Staphylococci* and *Streptococci*. He also stated that penicillin seemed to have no toxic effect on regular tissue or defense functions. After this initial paper, Fleming did very little other research with penicillin, and the medical and scientific communities generally ignored his observations.

In 1938, a team of scientists lead by Florey and Chain organized a research project that included work on penicillin. The group did extensive testing on the effects of penicillin, and studied its medical uses. After establishing the effectiveness of penicillin for fighting bacterial infections, the team worked to produce quantities of penicillin for medical treatment.

By 1945, Florey and Chain's work on penicillin production was complete. By the time World War II ended, enough penicillin could be produced for military needs. Production then expanded to provide penicillin to the civilian market.

Today, penicillin is considered one of the most important drugs to be developed in human history. It is still the best treatment for many bacterial infections.

EVALUATION   *Review the information you have been given about the development of penicillin. Then research and answer the following questions.*

1. What type of disease is penicillin effective against?

_____

_____

_____

2. Do you think Fleming should be credited with the discovery of penicillin? Why or why not? Write a paragraph discussing your point of view.

_____

_____

_____

_____

_____

_____

_____

_____

_____

Vocabulary Review

From each group of terms, choose the term that does not belong and then explain your choice.

1. hyphae, septa, lichen, mycelium

_____

_____

2. athlete's foot, ringworm, Dutch elm disease, measles

_____

_____

3. stolons, rhizoids, sac fungi, sporangia

_____

_____

4. rhizoids, basidia, zygospores, asci

_____

_____

5. sac fungus, yeast, mold, club fungus

_____

_____

6. stalk, cap, gills, conidia

_____

_____

7. morels, yeast, mildew, mushrooms

_____

_____

8. regeneration, hyphae, spores, budding

_____

_____

9. mycorrhizae, mildew, mushrooms, morels

_____

_____

10. zygomycota, ascomycota, basidiomycota, deuteromycota

_____

_____

Fungi
Chapter 16

. . . .

Test A

Choose the best answer for each question and write its letter on the line provided.

_____ **1.** Which of the following does *not* depend on the action of fungi?
       a. bread   **b.** soy sauce   **c.** toothpaste   **d.** antibiotics

_____ **2.** Fungi differ from plants in that they do not reproduce by seeds, and the cell walls of almost all fungi contain
       a. chitin   **b.** chloroplasts   **c.** chlorophyll   **d.** cellulose

_____ **3.** What organism digests and absorbs nutrients from dead organisms?
       a. mycelium   **b.** saprophyte   **c.** fruiting body   **d.** septa

_____ **4.** The tiny tubes filled with cytoplasm and nuclei that form the body of a fungus are called
       a. hyphae   **b.** rhizoids   **c.** fruiting bodies   **d.** mycelia

_____ **5.** Which of the following are *not* sac fungi?
       a. bird's nest fungi   **b.** unicellular yeasts   **c.** mushrooms   **d.** morels

_____ **6.** Septa are the walls that divide some
       a. mycorrhizae   **b.** stolon basidia   **c.** mycelia   **d.** hyphae

_____ **7.** A zygospore of a fungus is a resting state that contains a sporangium which produces many
       a. parasites   **b.** spores   **c.** nuclei   **d.** cysts

_____ **8.** Hyphae tangle and interweave to form a mass known as a
       a. mycelium   **b.** basidium   **c.** rhizoid   **d.** fruiting body

_____ **9.** By fusing their nuclei and through meiosis, spores of sac fungi form a(n)
       a. basidium   **b.** stolon   **c.** septum   **d.** ascus

_____ **10.** What fungus is used to make soy sauce and citric acid?
       a. *Penicillium*   **b.** *Aspergillus*   **c.** *Rhizopus*   **d.** *Candida*

_____ **11.** Bread mold and mildew are
       a. imperfect fungi   **b.** club fungi   **c.** common molds   **d.** sac fungi

_____ **12.** In mycorrhizae, the plant benefits from a fungus because the fungus
       a. keeps organic matter from breaking down
       b. acts as a parasite
       c. prevents the secretion of digestive enzymes
       d. breaks down organic matter in the soil

_____ **13.** The spore-producing structures of fungi are called
       a. fruiting bodies   **b.** mycelia   **c.** septa   **d.** lichen

_____ **14.** Stolons are hyphae that connect groups of
  a. spores
  b. bracket fungi
  c. mycelia
  d. rhizoids

_____ **15.** A lichen is a symbiotic association between a fungus and what organism?
  a. protist
  b. photosynthetic organism
  c. button mushroom
  d. mycorrhizae

_____ **16.** What is a familiar club fungus?
  a. rhizoid
  b. mold
  c. mushroom
  d. *Arthrobotrys*

_____ **17.** The process by which a smaller cell breaks away from a larger cell in some yeasts is called
  a. budding
  b. fusion
  c. conjugation
  d. fertilization

_____ **18.** Fungi that do not undergo sexual reproduction are known as
  a. sac fungi
  b. imperfect fungi
  c. common molds
  d. club fungi

_____ **19.** Mycorrhizae result from symbiotic relationships between fungi and what?
  a. protozoa
  b. animals
  c. plant leaves
  d. plant roots

_____ **20.** Millions of American elm trees have been killed by a sac fungus that acts both as a parasite and as a(n)
  a. decomposer
  b. photosynthesizer
  c. yeast
  d. imperfect fungus

_____ **21.** Fungi that feed on living hosts can be parasites, mutualistic partners, or
  a. saprophytes
  b. autotrophs
  c. predators
  d. zygospores

_____ **22.** Fungi are grouped into divisions based primarily on their
  a. method of reproduction
  b. cell structure
  c. ways of getting nutrients
  d. appearance

_____ **23.** What are the reproductive cells of fungi called?
  a. buds
  b. rhizoids
  c. hyphae
  d. spores

_____ **24.** Specialized hyphae that absorb nutrients and anchor common molds to their food source are called
  a. asci
  b. rhizoids
  c. stolons
  d. sporangia

_____ **25.** What structures in club fungi produce spores?
  a. stolons
  b. zygospores
  c. basidia
  d. asci

Fungi
Chapter 16

• •

Test B

Read each question or statement and respond on the lines provided.

1. a. What are the three most important structural characteristics of most fungi? *(15 points)*

_____

_____

b. How do most fungi obtain nutrients? *(5 points)*

_____

_____

_____

2. Account for the extremely rapid growth of most fungi. What structural characteristic enables such rapid growth? *(15 points)*

_____

_____

_____

_____

3. Complete the following table, which shows the characteristics of the four divisions of fungi. In each case, give the common name of the division (club fungi, common molds, imperfect fungi, or sac fungi). Then state how the fungi in that division typically reproduce (sexual, asexual, or both). Finally, give an example of a fungus in that division. *(24 points)*

Division	Common Name	Main Form of Sexual Reproduction	Example of Organism
a. Ascomycota			
b. Deuteromycota			
c. Zygomycota			
d. Basidiomycota			

4. State which type of fungi makes use of each of the following reproductive structures. *(15 points)*

a. zygospore

_____

b. ascus

_____

c. basidium

_____

5. a. Describe the symbiosis that occurs in lichens. *(6 points)*

_____

_____

_____

b. Describe the symbiosis that occurs in mycorrhizae. *(6 points)*

_____

_____

_____

c. Which relationship is mutually beneficial to both participating organisms? *(2 points)*

_____

_____

6. Suppose you were involved in a debate over whether fungi should be considered beneficial or harmful. Give three pieces of evidence to support each point of view. *(12 points)*

_____

_____

_____

_____

_____

_____

_____

_____

_____

Unit 4

Lab Practical Exam

14

•••

Goal

At this station, you will demonstrate two methods of inhibiting the growth of bacteria.

Materials

mock fluid from raw chicken   hot plate   liquid germicidal soap   water
4 beakers   stirring rod   pot holders   plastic wrap   labeling tape and marker

Safety

1. Wear safety goggles, laboratory aprons, and rubber gloves for this procedure. Use pot holders to handle hot beakers.

2. Work carefully to avoid spilling mock chicken fluid. When finished, pour the mock chicken fluid down the sink drain. Use germicidal soap to clean the sink and all equipment.

3. Throw out gloves and cleaning materials in a lined trash can. Place aprons in a lined laundry basket. Wash hands thoroughly with soap.

Procedure

Using only the materials provided, demonstrate two methods for inhibiting bacteria growth. List the steps for each method in the table.

Procedure 1	Procedure 2
1.	1.
2.	2.
3.	3.
4.	4.

Analyze Your Results

1. What methods did you use to inhibit bacterial growth in the chicken fluid?

_____

_____

2. Make a prediction about the outcome you would expect from each of the methods.

_____

_____

3. How can you apply the likely outcome of your experiment to preparing chicken for a meal?

_____

_____

_____

Unit 4

Lab Practical Exam

15

. . . .

Goal

You will analyze the results of an experiment that tested methods for inhibiting and encouraging algae growth.

Materials

four beakers containing:

   1% solution of plant fertilizer with phosphates and algae
   1% solution of plant fertilizer without phosphates and algae
   1% solution of chlorine bleach and algae
   pond water and algae

Safety

1. Wear safety goggles and laboratory aprons for this procedure.

2. Report all spills immediately.

Procedure

Observe the four samples of *Spirogyra* that were grown in different solutions for the same amount of time. Record your observations.

_____

_____

_____

_____

Analyze The Results

1. What variables were tested in this experiment?

_____

_____

2. Which of the substance(s) added to the algae inhibited growth? Which substance(s) encouraged growth? How do you know?

_____

_____

3. Based on the results of the experiment, describe the possible environmental impact of introducing phosphate products into streams or lakes.

_____

_____

4. Why do you think chlorine is added to the water in swimming pools?

_____

_____

Unit 4
Lab Practical Exam

16

Goal

At this station, you will analyze the results of an experiment that tested the role of yeast and preservatives in the formation of mold spores.

Materials

Four plastic zipper bags containing bread with yeast, bread without yeast, yeast bread with preservatives, and yeast bread without preservatives.

Safety

1. Wear eye goggles during the procedure.

2. Handle the plastic bags carefully.

3. Avoid opening plastic bags when you make observations.

Procedure

Observe the samples of bread that were moistened and exposed to the air several days ago. Record your observations.

_____

_____

_____

_____

Analyze The Results

1. What variables were tested in this experiment?

_____

_____

2. Describe what effect, if any, yeast has on the growth of mold on bread.

_____

_____

_____

3. Describe what effect, if any, preservatives have on the growth of mold on bread.

_____

_____

_____

Teacher's Notes
▪ ▪

Lab Practical Exam 14

Set up the station by preparing the following: Students will set up the demonstration, and answer questions about the set up.

- four test tubes each containing 25 mL of mock chicken fluid (dilute bullion and a very small amount of red food dye)
- test tube with 25 mL of germicide soap

SAFETY

Tell students that they should always wear laboratory aprons, goggles, and gloves when working with bacteria. Remind students to use pot holders to handle hot beakers. When finished, remind students to clean equipment and station surfaces with germicidal soap or alcohol and to wash their hands. Have students pour chicken fluid down a sink drain and clean the sink. You may want to inform the students that the mock chicken fluid used in the lab practical is actually not hazardous.

PROCEDURE

- Remind students to stir the soap and chicken fluid mixture.

Lab Practical Exam 15

Set up the station by preparing four labeled beakers that contain the following:

- 1% solution of plant fertilizer with phosphates and *Spirogyra* stock culture
- 1% solution of plant fertilizer without phosphates and *Spirogyra* stock culture
- 1% solution of chlorine bleach and *Spirogyra* stock culture
- solution of pond water, or aged tap water, and *Spirogyra* stock culture

Allow the algae to grow in the beakers for several days before conducting this lab practical.

SAFETY

Tell students that they should always wear laboratory aprons and goggles when working with liquid chemicals in the lab. Remind them to wash immediately if any of the substances come in contact with their skin.

Lab Practical Exam 16

MATERIALS

- 1 slice yeast bread
- 1 slice bread without yeast
- 1 slice yeast bread with preservatives
- 1 slice yeast bread without preservatives
- 4 plastic zipper bags
- spray bottle with water
- dark towel
- heat lamp

Set up the station by preparing the following: Moisten each bread slice slightly with the spray bottle. Place each slice of bread in a plastic zipper bag. Place the bags with bread on the dark towel under the heat lamp for two to three days.

SAFETY

- Tell students to wear eye goggles during the procedure.
- Suggest that they use care when handling the plastic bags.
- Tell students not to open the plastic bags.

Answer Key

Section Review 14.1
PART A
1. **a.** spikelike projections
   b. RNA
   c. envelope
2. **a.** protein coat that surrounds the nucleic acid core of a virus
3. protein
4. lipids, proteins, carbohydrates
5. nucleic acids; DNA or RNA
6. Spikes enable viruses to chemically recognize and attach to the cells they infect.

PART B
1. c
2. b
3. e
4. d
5. a

PART C
1. When the nucleic acid of a bacterial virus is attached to a host's chromosome, it is called a prophage.
2. The cell bursts, releasing its contents.
3. During the lytic cycle, the nucleic acid of the virus takes control of the activity of the cell. Viral DNA forces the host cell to produce viral DNA and proteins. The original host cell then lyses, releasing virus particles that attach to other cells, starting the process again. During the lysogenic cycle, the host cell reproduces normally. The phage DNA attaches to the bacterial chromosome and becomes an inactive prophage. The infected host cell may reproduce many times—each time reproducing the prophage. Eventually, because of outside stimuli, the virus starts the lytic cycle, replicates itself, and kills the host cell.

Interpreting Graphics 14
PART A
1. Students should label the first diagram Lytic Cycle and the second diagram Lysogenic Cycle.
2. Students should label Figure 2 as follows: g. 1, a. 2, e. 3, d. 4, c. 5, b. 6
3. Students should circle step c in Figure 2.

PART B
1. The bacteriophage attaches to the bacterial cell wall. The bacteriophage injects its DNA into the host cell. The bacteriophage DNA forces the host cell to produce new bacteriophage DNA and proteins. Bacteriophage DNA and proteins assemble into new virus particles. Bacteriophage enzymes lyse host cell wall, releasing virus particles.
2. In the lytic cycle, the virus takes over the cell and destroys the host cell in the process of viral replication. In the lysogenic cycle, the viral DNA attaches to the host cell chromosome, becomes a prophage, and is duplicated with the host cell chromosome for a number of division cycles. Eventually the viral DNA enters the lytic cycle and destroys the host cell in the process of viral replication.

Section Review 14.2
PART A
1. Beijerinck discovered tobacco mosaic disease was contagious. He also suggested that TMV was likely to be caused by unusually small bacteria.
2. Ivanovsky tested Mayer's hypothesis. Like Beijerinck, he concluded that tobacco mosaic disease was caused by unusually small bacteria.
3. Stanley isolated the tobacco mosaic virus and confirmed the work of Beijerinck. Stanley determined that a virus is made of nucleic acid and protein.

PART B
1. tobacco mosaic virus
2. transmission electron microscope
3. The word *virus* means poison. Viruses typically cause diseases in the organisms they enter.
4. Viruses began as fragments of chromosomes that came from specific organisms. The chromosome fragments escaped from their original cells and came to occupy host cells. Within host cells, the chromosome fragments replicated in the same way as host chromosomes. Eventually, the chromosome fragments evolved the ability to cause their host cells to make capsids that protected the nucleic acid strands when moving from cell to cell.

PART C
a. RNA
b. reverse transcriptase
c. envelope
d. core
e. envelope protein

PART D
1. Viroids are particles of pure RNA that cause diseases in plants. Prions are particles of protein that cause diseases in some animals.
2. Unlike viruses, viroids have no protein capsids. Prions lack the nucleic acids present in viruses.
3. A retrovirus replicates in a way opposite from the standard way that most viruses replicate. Retroviruses make DNA from RNA instead of making RNA from DNA.

Section Review 14.3
PART A
1. Likely responses will include any three of the following: smallpox, polio, measles, AIDS, mumps, influenza, yellow fever, rabies, or the common cold.
2. Likely responses will include any three of the following: rabies, pneumonia, fevers, pox, brain diseases, or scrapie.
3. A weakened virus is injected into a person to stimulate the body to produce specific cells and proteins to combat the virus. If a similar virus enters the person's body, the virus is destroyed by the special cells and proteins.

PART B
Viruses sometimes pick up pieces of host cell genes and carry them into other cells. Under controlled conditions, genetic engineers can correct genetic defects by using viruses to carry desirable genes from one cell to another.

Answer Key

∎∎∎

Critical Thinking 14

1. The assumption that all bacteria are microscopic organisms.

2. Due to this assumption, scientists focused on classifying the organism as either an algae or a protozoan.

3. Answers will vary but may include questions about how the unicellular organism exists without the sophisticated transport structures and cellular organization common to eukaryotes.

Enrichment Topic 14-1

Models may vary. Active immunity models should show how the antigen provokes antibody production. Passive immunity models should show antibodies being injected.

Section Review 14.4

PART A
1. a   4. d
2. b   5. e
3. f   6. c

PART B
1. f   4. c
2. a   5. b
3. d   6. e

PART C
1. a. chromosomes replicate
   b. chromosomes move to opposite ends of the cell
   c. cell divides
   d. two new, identical cells are produced
2. In binary fission, the DNA in the new cells is an exact copy of the parent cell's DNA. In conjugation, DNA is passed from one cell to another through cell-to-cell contact. During this process, genetic information is exchanged, so offspring are not exactly like either parent.
3. conjugation and transformation

Section Review 14.5

PART A
1. Archaebacteria: methanogens, extreme halophiles, extreme thermophiles
2. Eubacteria: cyanobacteria, chlamydias, gram positive, proteobacteria, spirochetes

PART B
1. Archaebacteria is a group of bacteria that live in unusually harsh environments and have features that are chemically distinct from other monerans.
2. Eubacteria are all the organisms traditionally known as bacteria.
3. Thermophiles are archaebacteria that live in extremely hot water.
4. Extreme halophiles are archaebacteria that live in extremely salty conditions.
5. Chemosynthesizers are archaebacteria that use inorganic compounds as energy sources.
6. Methanogens are archaebacteria that produce methane.

PART C
1. Gram-positive bacteria have a thick wall composed of a protein-sugar complex that turns purple during the Gram-staining process. Gram-negative bacteria have an extra lipid layer on the outside of the cell wall that turns pink during Gram-staining.
2. Scientists have studied the proteins, DNA, and RNA of living monerans and inferred their probable evolutionary relationships based on these studies.

PART D
1. composition of the cell wall; the presence of flagella; cell shape
2. The composition of the cell wall determines the reaction of monerans to the Gram-staining procedure, so Gram-staining can be used to identify the chemical composition and likely structure of the cell wall of a bacterium.
3. Heterotrophs receive their energy from organic molecules made by other organisms. Autotrophs make their own food from inorganic molecules and sunlight.
4. Chemoautotrophs obtain their energy from inorganic substances. Photoheterotrophs use sunlight for energy.

PART E
Check students' drawings for logic and accuracy. Be sure that students include membrane-bound organelles in the animal and plant cells and have not included them in the moneran cell.

Section Review 14.6

PART A
1. Decomposers are organisms that break down organic material.
2. Symbiosis is a relationship between two different kinds of organisms.
3. Bioremediation is the process of using microorganisms to help restore natural environmental conditions.

PART B
1. Likely responses will include pneumonia, diphtheria, tuberculosis, and Lyme disease. Accept all logical responses.
2. One strain that causes anthrax and one that causes tuberculosis.
3. A likely response will include bacteria living in the intestines of cows. The bacteria help the cow by breaking down the cellulose in the plants the cow eats, making nutrients available for the cow. The bacteria benefit by having a warm, safe environment in which to live.
4. Likely responses will include that humans use bacteria to tan leather, make vitamins, make vinegar, make antibiotics, make yogurt, make cheese, and to make sauerkraut.

Enrichment Topic 14-2

1. Acid-fast bacteria resist Gram staining and decolorization, so they are difficult to classify. They also have high lipid content.
2. Answers may vary. For example, the bacteria that causes leprosy is in the genus *Mycobacterium*. It forms colonies of branching chains that look like fungi.

Answer Key

■ ■

Vocabulary Review 14

1. pili; not a group of monerans
2. infection; not a form of reproduction
3. endospore; not a part of a virus
4. virus; not a name for Monera
5. moneran; a living thing, unlike others
6. cocci; a shape of monerans, not viruses
7. binary fission; not a process of virus replication
8. cyanobacteria; a group of eubacteria, not archaebacteria
9. aerobe; a form of respiration, not a way of obtaining nutrition
10. Sickle-cell disease; disorder not caused by virus or bacteria

Chapter 14 Test A

1. a	14. b
2. b	15. b
3. c	16. a
4. d	17. d
5. c	18. b
6. a	19. a
7. a	20. c
8. b	21. b
9. a	22. c
10. a	23. d
11. a	24. a
12. b	25. b
13. a	

Chapter 14 Test B

1. Figures 1 and 2 are viruses; Figure 3 is a moneran.
   a. tail fibers
   b. polyhedral capsid
   c. DNA or RNA
   d. spikelike projections
   e. DNA or RNA
   f. envelope
   g. chromosome
   h. cell membrane
   i. cytoplasm
   j. cell wall
   k. pili
   l. flagellum
2. Living: They reproduce themselves and contain nucleic acid and proteins. Nonliving: Outside of cells, they cannot reproduce, grow, move, or respire.
3. Bacteriophages were fragments of chromosomes in organisms. They escaped, occupied other cells, replicated there, and evolved the ability to make their host cells produce capsids. This allowed the viruses to move from cell to cell. Evidence includes the complete dependence of viruses on living hosts, the specificity of viruses, and the greater degree of similarity between viral and host genes than between the genes of different families of viruses.
4. Answers will vary. Compare student responses with figure 14.3 on pages 328 and 329 in the student edition.

5. Standard: contains DNA, which then makes cell produce proteins and copies of itself, which are reassembled to make new viruses. Retrovirus: contains RNA, releases enzyme to cause cell to make viral DNA from RNA. DNA makes RNA, which can be used directly to assemble viruses.
6. a. either; either; living   d. neither; both; living
   b. plants; RNA; nonliving   e. either; both; living
   c. animals; neither; living

Section Review 15.1

PART A

1. The ameba, *Euglena,* and *Paramecium* each have some type of nucleus and membrane-bound organelles. Monerans do not have nuclei or membrane-bound organelles.
2. The ameba and *Paramecium* have no chloroplasts or cell walls. Students may also note that they both the ameba and *Paramecium* have structures that enable them to move. Plant cells have chloroplasts, cell walls, and no structures for locomotion.
3. The *Euglena* is similar to a plant cell because it has chloroplasts. The *Euglena* differs from a plant cell because it has a flagellum and does not have a cell wall.
4. The *Euglena* is different from an animal cell because it has chloroplasts.
5. All have some type of nucleus and membrane-bound organelles, lack cell walls, and have specialized structures for movement.
6. Accept all logical responses. Likely responses include: Protists are eukaryotes with nuclei and other membrane-bound organelles. Some protists contain chloroplasts; others do not.

PART B

1. –	6. +
2. +	7. +
3. +	8. +
4. +	9. +
5. –	10. +

PART C

1. water
2. eukaryotes
3. colony
4. diversity
5. animal-like, plantlike, and funguslike

Section Review 15.2

PART A

1. c	5. a
2. d	6. g
3. f	7. e
4. b	

PART B

1. foraminiferans
2. pseudopods
3. ameba
4. cyst
5. contractile vacuole

Answer Key

∎ ∎

6. amebic dysentery
7. *Paramecium*
8. *Plasmodium*

PART C
1. Protozoans are classified based on how they move.
2. Sarcodinians move by extending lobes of cytoplasm called pseudopods. Ciliates are covered with cilia, short, hairlike projections that beat like oars to propel the ciliate through the water. Zooflagellates move by means of flagella.
3. *Trichonympha* lives in the gut of the termite and digests the cellulose in the wood that the termite eats. The *Trichonympha* then releases nutrients from the wood that the termite can absorb.

Interpreting Graphics 15
PART A
1. pseudopods
2. micronucleus, macronucleus, gullet, oral groove, anal pore, cilia
3. chloroplasts, flagellum

PART B
1. The ameba and the *Paramecium* are considered to be animal-like because they can locomote and do not carry out photosynthesis.
2. The *Euglena* is considered to be animal-like because it can locomote and take in nutrients from the outside. It is considered plantlike because it has chloroplasts and can carry out photosynthesis.
3. Answers will vary. Likely answers will include a means of locomotion, cytoplasm, nuclei.
4. The micronucleus controls reproduction. The macronucleus controls all other cell functions.

Section Review 15.3
PART A
1. Some protists are considered plantlike because they perform photosynthesis.
2. Algae contain chlorophyll, and produce food and oxygen as a result photosynthesis.
3. Unlike plants, algae do not contain specialized tissues or organs.
4. Algae are classified on the basis of differences in their structures.
5. Algae are divided into unicellular and multicellular algae.
6. Multicellular algae are classified according to color.

PART B
1. saltwater habitat
2. two flagella that spin the organism in a corkscrew fashion
3. diatoms
4. Shells have a huge variety of shapes.
5. Euglenoids
6. move using flagella
7. Chlorophyta, or green algae
8. Rhodophyta, or red algae
9. Phaeophyta, or brown algae

PART C
1. Red algae have accessory pigments in their chloroplasts that enable them to absorb the wavelengths of light that reach the deep ocean. The algae adjust the ratio of accessory pigments in response to reduced light.
2. Giant kelp have special air bladders. These bladders keep the leaflike portions of the kelp close to the surface so they can absorb sunlight.
3. Alternation of generations is the term for the complex life cycles of organisms in which organisms alternate a spore-producing stage and a gamete-producing stage.

Section Review 15.4
PART A
1. shiny, wet appearance; form multinucleate mass called a plasmodium
2. when feeding, function as a single cell with multiple nuclei
3. alternate between an ameboid form and a spore-producing fruiting body
4. form a pseudoplasmodium when food or water is scarce
5. cell walls are mostly cellulose; asexual reproduction produces spores with flagella
6. act as decomposers or parasites

PART B
1. Most funguslike protists are small and live in damp or watery places. They act as decomposers, helping to break down dead organic matter.
2. Plasmodial slime molds have a two-stage life cycle. In the feeding stage, a single cell with many nuclei called a plasmodium forms. When food becomes scarce, fruiting bodies that produce haploid spores appear. The haploid spores fuse to form a diploid zygote which develops into a new plasmodium.
3. A pseudoplasmodium is the multicellular, haploid form of a cellular slime mold; a true plasmodium is unicellular and diploid.
4. Both fungi and water molds have cell walls and produce spores. However, the cell walls in fungi contain chitin, while those of water molds are mostly cellulose. The spores produced by water molds have flagella; the spores of true fungi do not.

Critical Thinking 15
1. food source, mobility, presence of nuclei, and multicellularity
2. Answers will vary, but should include references to motility and food sources.
3. Answers may vary. For example, students could classify algae according to pigment, or the way they move and ingest food.
4. Euglenoids live mostly in fresh water, are unicellular, and have chloroplasts and one flagellum. Diatoms are unicellular, have shells made of silica, and have no flagella. Red algae are multicellular, have no flagella, and are mostly marine. Green algae are found in a wide range of habitats, have chloroplasts, and can be either unicellular or multicellular. Dinoflagellates are unicellular, have two flagella,

Answer Key

■ ■

chloroplasts, and cellulose plates for structure. Brown algae are almost entirely marine, include kelp, are multicellular and have anchoring structures called holdfasts.

Section Review 15.5
PART A
1. Plankton are the mostly microscopic organisms that float near the surface of oceans and lakes.
2. Phytoplankton are the photosynthesizing algae in plankton.
3. Phytoplankton are an important food source for whales and other heterotrophs. Phytoplankton also carry out more than 70 percent of Earth's photosynthesis, helping to keep oxygen and carbon dioxide levels in balance.
4. Three complex carbohydrates used in food products—carrageenan, agar, and algin—are extracted from seaweed.
5. The kinds and presence of protists in an ecosystem can indicate the health of the ecosystem.

PART B
1. e   5. f
2. g   6. b
3. a   7. d
4. c   8. h

PART C
1. b   4. a
2. d   5. c
3. e

Enrichment Topic 15-1
1. Answers may vary. Students may find that the rat flea, *Xenopsylla cheopis,* carried bubonic plague during the pandemics in the Middle Ages. The flea probably got the bacteria from the skin of an infected animal. The bacteria multiplied in the flea's upper digestive tract and eventually obstructed its digestive tract. When the flea fed on a human, the obstruction caused the blood it ingested to be regurgitated back into the bite, along with some bacteria. The flea also transmitted bacteria among rats or other animals in the same way.
2. Answers will vary, but students will probably find that the plague bacillus is still harbored by rats and fleas.

Vocabulary Review 15
1. protozoans
2. pseudopods
3. flagella
4. cilia
5. algae
6. alternation of generations
7. plankton
8. plasmodium
Scrambled letters: r, n, p, d, g, i, i, a, t, o, o, k, t, s, m
Solution: kingdom Protista

Chapter 15 Test A
1. a   14. d
2. b   15. b
3. d   16. c
4. c   17. a
5. b   18. c
6. a   19. b
7. d   20. d
8. b   21. a
9. c   22. d
10. a   23. c
11. d   24. a
12. b   25. d
13. c

Chapter 15 Test B
1. a. All protists are eukaryotic organisms.
   b. The incredible diversity of their size, shape, color, and manner of movement make the classification of protists difficult.
2. a. animals; heterotrophic
   b. plants; autotrophic
   c. fungi; decomposers
3. The sarcodinians, such as the ameba, move using pseudopods. The zooflagellates, such as *Trichonympha,* move using flagella. Ciliophorans, such as the paramecia, move using cilia. Sporozoans such as *Plasmodium* cannot move at all.
4. a. euglenoids
   b. red algae
   c. diatoms
   d. brown algae
   e. dinoflagellates
   f. green algae
5. a. The three groups are: plasmodial slime molds, cellular slime molds, and water molds.
   b. Responses may include: Plasmodial slime molds have single cells with multiple nuclei. Cellular slime molds have single ameboid cells. Water molds have cell walls that are mostly cellulose.
6. a. *Plasmodium* cause malaria, *Giardia* cause intestinal upset and nausea, and *Trypanosoma* cause African sleeping sickness.
   b. The protists in plankton are the base of the ocean food chain. Photosynthetic protists in plankton produce most of Earth's oxygen.

Section Review 16.1
PART A
1. b   4. a
2. e   5. c
3. d   6. f

PART B
Check students' diagrams for logic and accuracy. Sketches should show hyphae with septa and hyphae without cell walls. Students should label cell walls, cytoplasm, septa, and nuclei.

Answer Key

■ ■

PART C

1. One type of hyphae has septa, the other does not.
2. Fungal mycelia are able to grow quickly because hyphae absorb and breakdown organic molecules.
3. The three main parts of the body of a mushroom are the stipe (or stalk), the cap, and the annulus (marks the point of attachment of the cap to the stipe).
4. Fungi secrete enzymes into their environment, breaking down large, complex organic molecules into smaller molecules that can be readily absorbed.
5. Because a cluster of mushrooms is connected underneath the soil surface by a mat of mycelia, the mushrooms are actually part of a single organism.

Section Review 16.2

PART A

1. 400 million years ago
2. Fungi are grouped into a separate kingdom because they are significantly different from plants. Fungi have cell walls made of chitin, whereas plant cell walls are made of cellulose, and fungi cannot produce their own food as plants can.
3. Fungi are classified into four divisions based on their reproductive structures.
4. Imperfect fungi can only reproduce asexually; other types of fungi reproduce both sexually and asexually.
5. The four methods of asexual reproduction in fungi are cell division, budding, regeneration, and spore production.

PART B

1. g
2. f
3. c
4. e
5. b
6. d
7. a

PART C

1. asexual and sexual
2. ascus
3. morels, yeasts, powdery mildews
4. club fungi
5. basidia
6. green-headed jelly fungus, most mushrooms
7. common molds
8. asexual and sexual
9. bread mold, mildew
10. imperfect fungi
11. asexual
12. conidia

Interpreting Graphics 16

PART A

1. The classes are named for the reproductive structures of the organism.
2. spores
3. Asexual spores are produced at the tips of hyphae. Sexual spores form in the ascogonium.
4. They are two types of hyphae that are roughly analogous to male and female reproductive structures.
5. There are four ascospores produced as a result of meiosis and eight produced as a result of mitosis.

6. The imperfect fungi have no sexual reproductive structures. The other groups of fungi do.
7. The chromosome numbers are the same. Both are haploid.

Critical Thinking 16

1. Answers will vary but may include: How are spore cases strong enough to hold spores, but delicate enough to be broken by the wind? What is the chemical composition of a spore case? Why do only certain specialized hyphae make spore cases? How much pressure must be exerted on a spore case for it to break open? Does a spore case become more delicate as the number of spores it contains grows larger?
2. Accept all logical responses. Be sure students include a control in their experiment.
3. Questions should explore what would occur if a spore landed in an environment that lacked a basic requirement for fungal growth.
4. Accept all reasonable responses.

Enrichment Topic 16-1

1. Answers may vary. Reproduction in basidiomycetes is fairly complex. Most basidiomycetes have three stages of development. A basidiospore germinates and grows into a mycelium, septa form, and the hyphae are divided. Two mating types of hyphae conjugate, or self-fertilize. The paired nuclei in the fused hyphae divide, and new septa are formed.
2. Answers may vary. Basidiomycetes have clublike reproductive structures called basidia. They bear haploid spores. All basidiomycetes produce primary and secondary mycelium. Parental nuclei replicate by conjugate division.

Section Review 16.3

PART A

1. recycle; symbiotic
2. symbiosis
3. mutualistic; both organisms
4. photosynthetic organisms; fungus; photosynthetic organism

PART B

1. Fungi benefit from a mycorrhizal relationship because they absorb nutrients from the host plant.
2. Plants benefit from a mycorrhizal relationship because the fungi act as root extensions for the plant, increasing the plant's ability to absorb water and nutrients. In addition, the fungi break down large organic molecules, making nutrients more available to the plant.
3. Lichens can ____ extremely harsh environments because they ____ nthesis and absorb nutrients dissolve ____
4. Lichens b ____
5. rust, smut, Dut ____
6. As a parasite, the fun ____ a decomposer, it breaks down ____

PART C

1. used to make citric acid and soy sauce
2. used to make bread and ferment beverages
3. used to make an antibiotic

Answer Key

■ ■

Enrichment Topic 16-2

1. Penicillin is effective against infections caused by bacteria, including *Staphylococcus* and *Streptococcus*.

2. Answers may vary. Example: Florey and Chain did develop penicillin as a viable antibiotic drug, but they only knew about it from Fleming's research. Although he did not do further research on penicillin, Fleming did the initial research and published his results. Fleming was not the sole contributor, but neither were Florey and Chain. All three should share the credit for the development of penicillin as it is used today.

Vocabulary Review 16

1. Lichen. All others are structures of fungi.
2. Measles. All others are diseases caused by fungi.
3. Sac fungi. All others are specialized hyphae in common molds.
4. Rhizoids. All others are structures associated with reproduction in a fungus.
5. Yeast. All others are multicellular fungi.
6. Conidia. All others are visible parts of a mushroom.
7. Mushrooms. All others are examples of sac fungi.
8. Hyphae. All others are methods of reproduction in fungi.
9. Mycorrhizae. All others are saprophytes.
10. Deuteromycota. All others are phyla that reproduce sexually

Chapter 16 Test A

1. c	**14.** d
2. a	**15.** b
3. b	**16.** c
4. a	**17.** a
5. c	**18.** b
6. d	**19.** d
7. b	**20.** a
8. a	**21.** c
9. d	**22.** a
10. b	**23.** d
11. c	**24.** b
12. d	**25.** c
13. a	

Chapter 16 Test B

1. a. Fungi have cell walls made of chitin, they are composed of long thin tubules called hyphae, and the hyphae are interwoven to form mycelia.
   b. Most fungi are saprophytic, meaning that they absorb nutrients from dead or decaying organic matter.
2. The hyphae of fungal mycelia share the same cytoplasm. This characteristic permits rapid transport of nutrients to the areas of growth that need them most, resulting in rapid growth.
3. Examples for each division will vary.
   a. sac fungi; asexual usually; morels
   b. imperfect fungi; asexual; ringworm
   c. common molds; both; bread mold
   d. club fungi; sexual usually; mushroom

4. a. common molds
   b. sac fungi
   c. club fungi
5. a. Lichens are a symbiotic relationship between fungi and, usually, photosynthetic algae. The fungi obtain their food from the algae.
   b. Mycorrhizae are formed by a symbiotic relationship between fungi and plants. The fungi live in the roots of a plant, helping the plant to break down minerals in the soil for absorption. The fungi absorb nutrients made by the plant.
   c. Mycorrhizae are mutually beneficial to the fungi and the plant.
6. Responses may vary. To support the view that fungi are harmful, students may discuss fungal diseases that affect crops and trees, as well as fungal conditions affecting humans such as ringworm, athlete's foot, thrush, and mushroom poisoning. To support the view that fungi are beneficial, students may discuss edible fungi such as truffles and morels, the role of fungi in the making of cheese, medicines that are derived from fungi, and the use of yeasts in genetic engineering.

Lab Practical Exam 14

ANALYZE YOUR RESULTS

1. Answers may vary. Likely responses include heating the fluid and adding germicidal soap to the fluid.
2. Bacterial growth in the beaker that has been heated, and in the beaker to which germicidal soap has been added should be considerably less than a control beaker.
3. To prevent the growth of bacteria when cooking, you should be sure to cook the chicken thoroughly. To prevent contamination of other foods, clean all surfaces and utensils that came into contact with the raw chicken with germicidal soap.

Lab Practical Exam 15

PROCEDURE

Observations will vary. Students will likely note that algal growth was stimulated most in the beaker containing fertilizer with phosphates, and inhibited in the beaker with chlorine bleach.

ANALYZE YOUR RESULTS

1. The variables that were tested are the effects of different substances on algal growth.
2. Answers may vary. Students should find that chlorine inhibits growth and fertilizer with phosphates encourages growth. The control beakers for the chlorine and phosphate beakers should show intermediate levels of algae growth.
3. The introduction of fertilizers with phosphates could cause an increase in algae population, thereby upsetting the ecological balance of the lake or stream.
4. Chlorine inhibits the growth of algae and other protists that can make the water unattractive or unhealthy for swimmers.

Answer Key

Lab Practical Exam 16

PROCEDURE

Observations will vary. Students will notice that less mold grew on the bread without yeast, and on the bread with preservatives.

ANALYZE YOUR RESULTS

1. The variables that were tested were the effects of yeast and preservatives on bread mold growth.
2. Yeast encourages mold growth. Control bags showed that bread without yeast did not have the same amount of mold as the bread with yeast.
3. The growth of mold was inhibited by preservatives. Control bags showed that bread without preservatives had more mold.